M ANAGING
FINANCE

MANAGING FINANCE

CMI
Chartered
Management
Institute

P
PROFILE BOOKS

First published in Great Britain in 2014 by
Profile Books Ltd
3a Exmouth House
Pine Street
Exmouth Market
London EC1R 0JH
www.profilebooks.com

10 9 8 7 6 5 4 3 2 1

A CIP catalogue record for this book is available from the British Library.

ISBN: 978 1 78125 218 5
eISBN: 978 1 78125 217 8

Text design by sue@lambledesign.demon.co.uk

Typeset in Helvetica by MacGuru Ltd
info@macguru.org.uk

Printed and bound in Britain by Clays, Bungay, Suffolk

All reasonable efforts have been made to obtain permission to reproduce copyright material. Any omissions or errors of attribution are unintentional and will be corrected in future printings following notification in writing to the publisher.

About the checklist series

Management can be a daunting task. Managers are expected to provide direction, foster commitment, facilitate change and achieve results through the efficient, creative and responsible deployment of people and other resources. On top of that, managers have to manage themselves and develop their own personal skills. Just keeping up is a challenge – and we cannot be experts in everything.

The checklists in this series have been developed over many years by the Chartered Management Institute (CMI) to meet this challenge by addressing the main issues that managers can expect to face during their career. Each checklist distils good practice from industry to provide a clear and straightforward overview of a specific topic or activity, and has been reviewed by CMI's Subject Matter Experts Panel to reflect new research and changes in working life.

The series is designed both for managers who need an introduction to unfamiliar topics, and for those who want to refresh their understanding of the salient points. In more specialised areas – for example, financial management – checklists can also enable the generalist manager to work more effectively with experts, or to delegate more effectively to a subordinate.

Why is the checklist format useful? Checklists provide a logical, structured framework to help professional managers deal with an increasingly complex workplace – they help shape our thoughts and save us from being confused by too much information. At the same time, checklists help us to make good use of what we already know. They help us to remember things and prevent us from forgetting something important. Thus, no matter how expert we may already be, using checklists can improve outcomes and give us the confidence to manage more effectively, and to get the job done.

About this book

If you are in a managerial position and have to manage a budget or consider the financial consequences of your actions, *Managing Finance* is for you. Using a combination of action-oriented checklists and definitions, this book helps to demystify what is to many a daunting subject. The checklists cover the essential financial disciplines – understanding accounts, managing and monitoring, and tools for financial decision-making. For example, setting budgets and creating financial forecasts can help you anchor your expectations and keep a lid on costs. The checklists also equip you to understand the profit and loss statement, offering a guide to the conventional means of presenting financial performance during a trading period. In addition, this concise and indispensable handbook provides valuable guidance on gauging financial returns, with clear explanations of conventional terms such as return on investment and net present value, together with a sound introduction to more advanced tools of financial analysis such as return on assets and return on capital employed.

Alternative US and IAS accounting terms are also in use – see page xi for a short list.

Contents

Financial decisions

Introduction

For a core management discipline based largely upon factual data, finance can generate a surprising amount of emotion. Accountancy measures still form the core of the annual report, and a high proportion of chief executives have a background in finance. Yet the term 'bean-counter' is used in a pejorative sense, and at times businesses are accused of focusing too much on cost analysis, and not enough on innovation.

Not everyone has a natural aptitude for figures or calculations and some managers try to avoid the subject of finance as much as possible, or approach it with trepidation. Many lack formal training in financial management and may be embarrassed by their lack of understanding. But it is vital for managers to have a grasp of the basic principles of finance and accounting which will enable them to do their jobs effectively.

Finance is not the only measure of an organisation's success, but every manager should be able to interpret a balance sheet, know about cash flow, and make links between financial reports and other aspects of an organisation's performance. A comparison can be drawn with managers' approach to IT: it is a specialist area and not everyone can be a technical expert, but managers need to have a grasp of what the latest technology can do. It is the same with finance. Managers at all levels are involved in decision-making, business planning and project management. They need to assess the financial implications of differing courses of action and be aware of the financial consequences of the decisions they take. Furthermore, presentations that are financially literate will be more convincing and credible.

A grounding in accounting concepts and practices will also enable managers to engage in meaningful conversations with the finance department. Managers need to understand the financial position of the company and the implications for their own team or function, whilst accountants need to understand how managers' roles generate revenues for the organisation. Experience shows that strong partnerships, in which finance has a good understanding of how revenues and profits are generated and other functions take responsibility for budgets, proposals and financial reports in their area, are a feature of well-run companies.

Every organisation needs well-educated and well-rounded managers who can carry out their responsibilities competently. As one who has the privilege of investing in the education of future managers and leaders, I am convinced that management skills and knowledge can be taught and learned. Managers will always need to rely on the expertise of accountants and financial experts and it is important for them to understand when specialist knowledge is required and where to go for it. But managers also have a responsibility to broaden and develop their own knowledge and understanding.

I am therefore delighted to introduce this new title in the CMI checklist series on the subject of managing finance. The book is no substitute for a full financial education, but it offers a range of checklists introducing basic concepts of financial management and providing practical guidance on a range of financial tools and techniques.

Sir Paul Judge
Sheriff of the City of London

A note about accounting terms

These checklists were written in the UK and the pound (£) has been used as the base currency throughout.

The basic principles of accounting are similar around the world, but the UK and the US use a number of different terms, and there are also variations of terminology in the increasingly widely adopted International Accounting Standards (IAS). (These are also often referred to as International Financial Reporting Standards, or IFRS.) The following table lists some key UK and pre-IAS terms alongside examples of US and IAS variations. (Please note that this list is intended primarily to highlight differences; it does not provide definitive equivalents, and some terms are open to interpretation.)

UK/pre-IAS terms	US/IAS terms
Accounting period/year	Fiscal period/year
Balance sheet	Statement of financial position
Capital and reserves	Equity
Creditors	Payables
Debtors	Receivables
Financial accounts	Financial statements
Financial year	Fiscal year
Fixed assets	Property, plant and equipment
Gross profit	Gross income
Interest payable	Finance costs
Long-term liabilities	Non-current liabilities

UK/pre-IAS terms	US/IAS terms
Net profit	Profit for the year
Operating profit	Net income
Profit	Income
Profit and loss account	Income statement
Profit and loss balance	Retained earnings
Provision for bad debts	Allowance for bad debts
Sales or turnover	Revenue
Shares	Stock
Stock	Inventory

Reading a balance sheet

A balance sheet is a snapshot of a company's financial position at a given date. It differs from a profit and loss account, which summarises a company's trading performance during a given period. The date of the balance sheet is always disclosed in the heading and the figures are (or should be) correct as of that date.

This checklist is designed to help you read and understand a balance sheet. It is intended as a guide, not as a replacement for full accounting support and interpretation. While reference is made to UK legislation, guidance and practice, the principles outlined should also be helpful to readers in other financial jurisdictions.

Balance sheets should help to provide a thorough and detailed understanding of a company's financial position. They should indicate the solvency and liquidity of a company and may help predict impending financial difficulties. They may also be compared with earlier balance sheets to see how a company is progressing. There are good internal and legal reasons for producing a balance sheet, and it also provides information to assist creditors in assessing the creditworthiness of a company. In a nutshell, the balance sheet helps them answer the question: 'Can the company pay?'

Every balance sheet includes the balance of every account in the accounting system. Accounts are not usually shown individually, but those of a similar nature are grouped together to show just one net figure for each category. For example, there may be many accounts relating to fixed assets and accumulated depreciation, but just one net figure will be shown in the balance sheet. All the accounts of a profit and loss nature are aggregated to show a net profit or net loss. This is shown in the balance sheet as part of capital and reserves.

A balance sheet summarises the balances in a double-entry bookkeeping system and as a consequence it must balance. This means that the total of all the debit balances (assets) must equal the total of all the credit balances (liabilities). These totals always appear twice. The method of presentation usually shows some liabilities being deducted from the assets, but there are always two identical totals.

A company may produce a balance sheet for internal purposes; this may be done in any way chosen by the management and with any chosen date range. However, a balance sheet must also be prepared as at the last day of the company's financial year, which is the final date of the profit and loss period. This balance sheet is published and it must be drawn up in accordance with recognised statutory and accounting rules. Published accounts should include an auditor's report.

Alternative US and IAS accounting terms are also in use – see page xi for a short list.

Points to remember about balance sheets

- A balance sheet is always out of date. It shows figures obtained at some specified date in the past.

- Some of the figures may reflect subjective judgements. Examples are the bad debt reserve and the valuation of stocks.

- Some of the book values may differ from the 'real-life' realisable values. An example is the figure for fixed assets after accumulated depreciation.

Published balance sheets

An example of a balance sheet is shown on the following page, in a form suitable for publication. In the UK, the Companies Act 2006 requires that published balance sheets are shown in one of two specified formats: the horizontal format or the vertical format. Virtually all balance sheets are in the vertical format, and the example is shown in this way.

The Companies Act specifies a long list of headings that must be used. However, if there is a nil balance for a heading, it may be omitted. A balance sheet should also always be accompanied by explanatory notes. Comparative figures for the previous published balance sheet must also be given.

A balance sheet must be formally approved by the directors and signed by one of them. It must be sent to Companies House within nine months of the end of each accounting reference period (if it is a private company) or within six months (if it is a public company). The directors may take an extra three months if there are exports or overseas interests. A copy of the balance sheet of any company registered in the UK may be obtained by contacting Companies House.

Large public companies have to show a complete audit report. A company may be exempt from the requirement to have an audit when its turnover is less than £6.5 million and its balance sheet total is less than £3.26 million. It must also have 50 employees or fewer. For charities and charitable companies, there may be other legal requirements for audit and accounting. In the UK, the Charity Commission can provide details.

These exemption limits are constantly changing and the latest position should be checked with an accountant.

Example

ACME LTD
Balance sheet at 30 June 2013

	30 June 2012		30 June 2013	
	£	£	£	£
Fixed assets				
Tangible assets		2,398,834		2,450,804
Current assets				
Stocks	5,545,805		5,068,240	
Debtors	4,614,264		5,948,817	
Investments (short-term)	28,250		94,930	
Cash at bank and in hand	3,423		3,467	
	10,191,742		11,115,454	
Creditors: amount falling due within one year	(5,500,243)		(6,642,622)	
Net current assets		4,691,499		4,472,832
Total assets less current liabilities		7,090,333		6,923,636
Creditors: amounts falling due after more than one year		(747,665)		(918,458)
Provision for liabilities and charges		(20,855)		(37,100)
Net assets		6,321,813		5,968,078
Capital reserve				
Called up share capital		1,779,992		1,779,992
Revaluation reserve		620,240		634,200
Profit and loss account		3,921,581		3,553,886
Shareholders' funds		6,321,813		5,968,078

The financial statements were approved by the Board on ....
...............................Director
The notes on pages .... to .... form part of these financial statements.

Action checklist

1 Look at shareholders' funds

The balance sheet is set out showing the liabilities deducted from the assets. The amount left over, provided that the company is solvent, is the value that the owners have invested in it. In the example on page 4 this figure is £6,321,813. Shareholders' funds are split into share capital accounts, reserve accounts and profit and loss account. The profit and loss account represents the amount of profits that have been retained and not distributed to shareholders. Notes give further details. Again, using the example, if there are 1 million shares in issue, each has a net asset backing of £6.32.

2 Look at net current assets

Current assets are likely to be owned for less than a year or realisable in less than a year, and further details are usually given in the notes. They may include:

● short-term investments

● stocks

● money owed to the company (debtors)

● prepayments (payments, such as rent, made in advance)

● bank accounts in credit

● cash.

3 Look at current liabilities

Current liabilities are short-term debts due to be settled within the next year and further details are usually given in the notes. They may include:

● bank overdrafts and short-term loans

● money owed by the company (creditors)

● accruals (debts incurred where invoices have not yet been received).

4 Consider the figure for net current assets

This figure – which is an important one – is calculated by deducting current liabilities from current assets. The greater the figure, the greater is the margin of safety – with less chance of a funding crisis in the near future. There is nearly always a figure for net current assets, and a deficit is termed net current liabilities. This would be a cause for serious concern or, at the very least, indicate a need to ask some searching questions. In the example the figure is £4,691,499, which seems satisfactory.

5 Consider the liquidity ratio

This reflects the ability of a company to pay its debts as they fall due. It compares liquid assets to current liabilities. Liquid assets are cash, bank and debtors' balances. For example:

Cash	3,423
Debtors	4,614,264
Liquid assets	4,617,687
Creditors	5,500,243

The liquidity ratio is 0.84 (4,617,687/5,500,243). This is less than 1 and might mean that the company has difficulty in paying debts when they fall due. This may be an area for a further 'aged' analysis of debtors and creditors. On the face of it the company has little cash, even though it has strong retained earnings. Profit does not always equate to cash and many profitable companies get into trouble through poor cash management and overtrading.

6 Examine the fixed assets

Assets are items owned by the company, expressed in financial terms. 'Fixed assets' are those items of long-term value to a business and appear at the top of the balance sheet. They may be divided into three categories:

- tangible – land, buildings, plant, equipment, machinery, fixtures and fittings, motor vehicles
- intangible – licences, intellectual property, patents, goodwill

- investments – in other companies, government stocks.

  Fixed assets are likely to be long-term assets and are most likely to be items in which the company does not trade.

7 Consider the accounting policies

The key accounting policies are disclosed in the notes. The most important questions are likely to include:

- How are the stocks valued?
- What are the policies concerning depreciation of fixed assets?
- What are the policies concerning the bad debt reserve and other reserves?

Different accounting policies produce different profit or loss figures and a different balance sheet. A change in accounting policies may be important and must be disclosed in the notes.

As a manager you should avoid:

- forgetting that the assets are 'book values' and not necessarily what would actually be obtained in the event of a sale
- forgetting that a balance sheet is a snapshot on one particular day, and that it is out of date by the time it appears.

Reading a profit and loss statement

A profit and loss statement shows the summarised trading activity of a company or other organisation during a stated period and reflects all accounting entries of a profit and loss nature during that time. Profit and loss statements are frequently prepared for internal management purposes.

In the UK, companies and certain other organisations must publish profit and loss statements. The profit and loss statements of companies must, by UK law, comply with one of four formats. One of these is in more common use and is the one used in the example on page 10. Published profit and loss statements are almost always accompanied by detailed notes, and it is permissible to include some of the information in the notes rather than in the statement itself. Figures for the corresponding previous period are also shown.

A medium-sized company (as defined by the UK Companies Act and with certain exceptions) is permitted to show less information in its published profit and loss statement. A small company (as defined by the UK Companies Act and with certain exceptions) need not publish a profit and loss statement.

This checklist is intended to provide guidance on understanding profit and loss statements, but should not be seen as a replacement for full accounting support and interpretation.

A considered reading of a profit and loss statement can provide:

- a meaningful indication of the financial performance of the company for the period covered

- a thorough understanding of past performance – this is essential when drawing up future budgets and formulating plans
- a better understanding of other parts of the accounts and reports.

Action checklist

1 Look at the trends

In a published profit and loss statement, figures for the current and previous year are given. Key figures for additional periods may be elsewhere in the accounts. It is always worth looking at the trends revealed.

The example on the following page shows that turnover is up and profit is down, indicating a worsening in margins.

2 Look at the profit/turnover ratio

Profit on ordinary activities expressed as a percentage of turnover is generally considered to be one of the key ratios. Sometimes profit before tax is used and sometimes profit after tax. The trend in the ratios may be particularly significant. In the example:

If profit *before* tax is used, it is 9.8%: $\dfrac{98.2}{999.9}$

For the previous year it is 16.9%: $\dfrac{155.8}{923.6}$

If profit *after* tax is used, it is 7.7%: $\dfrac{77.1}{999.9}$

For the previous year it is 13.5%: $\dfrac{124.4}{923.6}$

Alternative US and IAS accounting terms are also in use – see page xi for a short list.

Example

ACME LTD
Consolidated profit and loss account for the year to
31 December 2013

	Year to 31 Dec. 2013	Year to 31 Dec. 2012
	£'000	£'000
Turnover	999.9	923.6
Cost of sales	(444.4)	(324.2)
Gross profit	555.5	599.4
Distribution costs	(161.8)	(138.7)
Administrative expenses	(322.2)	(299.0)
Other operating income	21.6	31.8
Income from shares in group undertakings	93.1	193.5
Income from participating interests	15.9	13.7
Income from other fixed asset investments	12.4	10.8
Other interest receivable and similar income	7.6	7.2
Amounts written off investments	(3.0)	(3.0)
Interest payable and similar charges	(27.8)	(66.4)
Profit on ordinary activities before taxation	98.2	155.8
Tax on profit on ordinary activities	(21.1)	(31.4)
Profit on ordinary activities after taxation	77.1	124.4
Non-controlling interests	(13.4)	(21.6)
	63.7	102.8
Other taxes not shown under the above items	(0.6)	(0.6)
Profit for the year	63.1	102.2
Dividends paid and proposed	(28.0)	(20.0)
Retained profit for the period	35.1	82.2

No items are now presented in the income statement as extraordinary items under IFRS (International Financial Reporting Standards) regulations, but they are permissible under US GAAP (generally accepted accounting principles). (IAS 1.87) Extraordinary items are unusual, abnormal and infrequent. What is 'unusual' would depend upon the country.

3 Look at the cost of sales percentage

This reveals the gross margin, which is the difference between turnover (or income) and the cost of goods manufactured or purchased.

It is particularly useful to look at the trend in the cost of sales percentage. Of course, like all the other ratios, consideration should be given to the reasons for the figures and the reasons for the changes. For example, a worsening in the ratio, although apparently unwelcome, may be the result of a management decision to boost sales by cutting prices and part of a plan to increase the overall net profit. In the example:

The cost of sales percentage is 44.4%: $\dfrac{444.4}{999.9}$

In the previous period it was 35.1%: $\dfrac{324.2}{923.6}$

So the gross profit margin has deteriorated.

4 Read the notes to the financial statement

It is almost certain that detailed notes will accompany a published profit and loss statement. They may well include further information in the following areas:

- a breakdown of turnover showing sales by region and type of product
- details of interest paid and interest received
- details of the tax charge
- details of dividends paid and proposed
- details of employee costs, repairs and renewals, the depreciation charge and the basis of its calculation.

5 Consider the profit and loss statement in conjunction with the rest of the accounts

Some useful ratios may be obtained by comparing figures from the profit and loss statement with figures from the balance sheet and elsewhere. One such ratio is return on capital employed (ROCE). If the example is used and if capital employed is £500,000:

ROCE for the current period is 15.4%: $\dfrac{77.1}{500.0}$

This uses 'profit on ordinary activities after taxation', though sometimes a different definition of profit may be used.

6 Be aware of the accounting policies

Many of the accounting entries leading to the profit and loss statement are matters of clear fact in that money has been received or spent. However, some of them may depend on judgement and the accounting policies used. Areas most likely to be affected include depreciation, bad debts, reserves and accounting for long-term contracts. Markedly different results may be obtained if different accounting policies are used.

In the case of a published profit and loss statement, the main accounting policies are stated in the notes. So too are any changes in the accounting policy and the effect of such changes.

7 Look at interest and dividends

These are the rewards for providing finance for a company. Dividends are paid to the owners (the shareholders) and in most cases the amount can vary from year to year; it can be nil. Interest is paid to banks and other providers of loans. Interest may be receivable as well as payable, if the company does not borrow.

Interest and dividends are important and both will be shown in a published profit and loss statement. Interest contributes to the profit or loss before tax. Dividends are an appropriation of profit and are shown after the figure for 'profit before tax'. In order to fully appreciate the figures it is necessary to study them in conjunction with the balance sheet and the notes. A relatively high interest payable figure may be a cause for concern. It may indicate that the company is overtrading and it may turn an otherwise acceptable profit into a disappointing profit, or even into a loss.

As a manager you should avoid:

- missing the significance of a change in accounting policy – for example, a change from 10% per year to 15% per year in writing down a £1,000,000 fixed asset reduces the declared annual profit by £50,000

- missing the significance of a change in the accounting period – for example, a 15-month period to 28 February includes two Christmases

- forgetting that there may be an explanation for odd-looking figures and ratios.

Business ratios

A business ratio is the quantitative relationship between two values in an organisation's financial statements.

Business ratios are used to quantify and explain many areas of business activity. They are used to compare the performance within a company between one period and another, for comparisons between companies, and to benchmark performance against industry and other norms. The analysis of business ratios highlights areas of business activity that need further examination and explanation. However, when studying business ratios care is needed to avoid jumping to a wrong conclusion and making an incorrect diagnosis. Try to keep things simple and always make sure when comparing your ratios with those of another analyst that you have both used the same method.

The stakeholders who use published accounts and ratio analysis to help them make decisions include shareholders, lenders, potential investors, suppliers, customers, employees and management. It must be remembered that published accounts provide only past information. Many stakeholders require much more up-to-date information such as interim accounts and management accounts. However, the same ratio analysis techniques can also be applied to these other sources of financial information. This checklist explains the commonly used ratios and uses the example financial statements below as a basis for calculating business ratios in order to obtain a better understanding of the company's performance.

Example

Profit and loss account for CM Ltd

	2013	2012
	£m	£m
Sales	700	750
Cost of sales (materials)	320	360
Gross profit	380 (54%)	390 (52%)
Expenses	120	140
Profit before interest and taxation	260	250
Interest	40	50
Profit before taxation	220	200
Taxation (30%)	66	60
Net profit after taxation	154	140
Dividends paid to shareholders	50	114
Profit retained	104	26

The gross profit as a percentage of sales in 2013 is 54%: 380/700. The gross profit percentage (sometimes called gross margin or contribution) is one of the most important business ratios.

Alternative US and IAS accounting terms are also in use – see page xi for a short list.

Ratio analysis

Ratios provide an understanding of financial performance and enable comparisons between periods and with other companies/industries. Using ratios you can determine efficiency and track trends in profitability, operational efficiency, financial gearing, liquidity and returns on investment.

1 Gross profit percentage (gross margin)

This important ratio is one that is often considered first in an analysis of business performance. It shows the ratio of gross profit to sales expressed as a percentage and is used in product profitability and contribution comparisons, often as an aid to sales price strategy.

Example

Balance sheet for CM Ltd

	2013	2012
	£m	£m
Fixed assets		
Plant & equipment (after depreciation)	190	190
Current assets		
Stocks of raw materials	300	350
Debtors	250	180
Cash at bank	60	70
Current liabilities		
Trade creditors	(260)	(290)
Bank overdraft	(150)	(210)
Net current assets	200	100
Total fixed and net current assets	390	290
Capital & reserves		
Called up share capital	250	250
Retained profits	140	20
Term loan	–	20
	390	290

Note that in 2013 the company no longer has a term loan. It has increased retained profits and net current assets.

In the example profit and loss account on page 15, for the year 2013 the gross profit was £380 million and sales were £700 million. The gross profit percentage is:

$$\frac{\text{Gross profit}}{\text{Sales}} \times \frac{100}{1}$$

$$\frac{£380m}{£700m} \times \frac{100}{1}$$

Gross profit percentage = 54% (to the nearest whole number)

This is an improvement on the previous year's gross profit of 52%. A stakeholder or analyst might compare these gross profit percentages with those achieved in other similar businesses.

The gross profit percentage is useful when comparing the contribution that individual product sales make towards a company's overall pool of fixed costs.

For example:

	Product A	Product B
Unit selling price	£8	£7
Unit variable cost of sales	£4	£2
Unit contribution (gross margin)	£4	£5
Gross margin as % of sales	50	71

A business may wish to maximise sales of product B since it makes a higher contribution to the fixed pool of overheads and profits. Price and volume decisions are generally much easier to understand on a marginal/contribution basis than they are if fixed costs are fully absorbed into product costs.

In the following example a company has three product lines: A, B and C. Budgeted selling prices, volumes and margins are as follows:

	A	B	C	Total
Unit selling price	£8	£7	£6	
Unit variable costs	£4	£2	£2	
Unit gross margin	£4 (50%)	£5 (71%)	£4 (67%)	
Volumes	100	100	100	
Total gross margin (contribution)	£400	£500	£400	£1,300
Fixed overheads	£500	£250	£250	£1,000
Profit/(loss)	(£100)	£250	£150	£300

Note that overheads have been allocated to products on the basis of their variable (production) costs. For example, product A is assumed to have absorbed 4/(4+2+2) of £1,000 of the total overheads.

On this basis product A is shown to have made a loss of £100. However, this does not necessarily mean that it should be dropped. The reason for this is that unless there is a more profitable product available to replace product A, dropping it only reduces the overall profit from £300 to create an overall loss of £100. Product A makes a contribution (another name for gross profit or gross margin) of £400. If product A is dropped, the £400 contribution towards the fixed pool of overheads will be lost. However, the fixed overheads will remain and will have to be allocated (absorbed) across the other two products.

This is why understanding gross profit and contribution is so important to decisions concerning selling prices, volumes and volume/mixes.

2 Net profit percentage

The net profit percentage compares net profit to sales. There are a number of definitions of net profit. The basic calculation for net profit percentage is as follows:

$$\frac{\text{Net profit}}{\text{Sales}} \times \frac{100}{1}$$

In the example profit and loss account for CM the net profit ratio for 2013 is:

$$\frac{£154}{£700} \times \frac{100}{1}$$

Net profit percentage = 22%

This ratio indicates that the net profit after interest and taxation is 22% of sales. Note that we have used net profit after interest and taxation. Other analysts might define net profit differently. Always make sure that you compare like with like. Another net profit ratio often quoted by analysts uses net profit before interest and taxation (NBIT).

3 Current ratio

This ratio measures the solvency of a business by comparing current assets with current liabilities. It is normally shown just as a single figure.

$$\text{Current ratio} = \frac{\text{Current assets}}{\text{Current liabilities}}$$

Using figures from the example balance sheet of CM for 2013:

Stock and work-in-progress	300
Debtors	250
Cash at bank	60
Total current assets	610
Trade creditors	(260)
Bank overdraft	(150)
Total current liabilities	(410)

$$\text{Current ratio} = \frac{610}{410}$$
$$\text{Current ratio} = 1.49$$

This is a positive number and it indicates that, on a going concern basis, the company is solvent. However, the company does have to collect its debts and convert its stock into sales and ultimately cash in order to be able to pay its creditors and bank overdraft.

Bank overdrafts are repayable on demand. So although this company has a positive current ratio it is not particularly liquid. Solvency does not always equal liquidity. There is a specific test of a company's liquidity, called the liquidity ratio.

4 Liquidity ratio

The liquidity ratio provides an indication of a company's ability to repay its debts as they fall due. It is usually expressed as a single figure, and a figure that is greater than 1 would indicate that the company is liquid and can readily pay off its debts. A ratio of less than 1 would indicate that the company might find it difficult to pay debts on time. Many profitable companies are not liquid and run into difficulties.

$$\text{Liquidity ratio} = \frac{\text{Liquid assets}}{\text{Current liabilities}}$$

Liquid assets are cash and debtors. Stock is not a liquid asset since it still has to be converted into a sale.

For CM the liquidity ratio for 2013 is:

$$\text{Liquidity ratio} = \frac{250 + 60}{260 + 150}$$

$$\text{Liquidity ratio} = 0.76$$

The liquidity ratio is less than 1 and this indicates that the company could have problems in repaying debts as they fall due. If the overdraft were called in, it would struggle. This gives the bank considerable leverage. Is this what the company wants or would it be better arranging some more long-term loan finance? Note that the company has repaid some term loan. Would it have been wiser to have kept the term loan and minimised the overdraft, thus increasing liquidity? There is more to finance than just obtaining the lowest cost of borrowing. The correct type of funding needs to be in place. As an alternative to obtaining more term loan, it might want to convert stocks more quickly into sales and reduce stock levels.

The company needs to collect cash from its own debtors before it can pay its creditors. It appears to be profitable, but it does need to make sure that it does not 'overtrade' and find itself without enough liquidity.

This ratio is useful in highlighting financial risk areas for management attention. The well-known saying that 'cash is king' is true – most failures are caused by cash and overall liquidity problems.

5 Stock turnover ratio

The stock turnover ratio is a measure of how fast stock moves through a business. A slow stock turnover is costly. Holding on to stocks results in increases in the costs of interest (on funds invested in stock), warehousing (rent, etc), obsolescence, damage and other holding costs.

However, it must also be remembered that there might be pricing benefits from buying larger quantities of stocks, and that having too low a level of stock might cause production flow problems or an inability to meet orders. An optimal level of stock needs to be determined by the stock controller.

The stock turnover ratio is an indicator of how fast stock moves. Notwithstanding the points mentioned above, a high stock turnover number would generally be considered healthy, since fewer funds were being tied up in stock. Stock turnover ratios calculated using year-end figures often conceal movements during the accounting period. The year-end value of stock may not reflect average stock values. This consideration also applies to other ratios that are calculated using year-end values. The calculation for stock turnover ratio normally uses average stock values:

$$\text{Stock turnover} = \frac{\text{Cost of sales (material costs only)}}{\text{Average stock values}}$$

Average stock value is calculated by adding the figure for stocks at the end of the year to the figure at the beginning of the year and dividing by two. So in the following example, the figure for CM stocks at the end of 2013 is added to the figure at the end of 2012 and divided by two.

$$\text{Average stock value} = \frac{300 + 350}{2}$$

$$\text{Average stock value} = 325$$

$$\text{Stock turnover} = \frac{320 \text{ (cost of sales, materials)}}{325 \text{ (average stock value)}}$$

$$\text{Stock turnover} = 0.98 \text{ times per year}$$

This stock turns over less than once a year and would normally be considered as very slow. However, what is fast or slow would depend upon the type of business CM is in. What are the industry benchmarks? Be careful not to jump to conclusions. However, if stock turnover cannot be increased, the company will need to consider how it funds such a slow turnover and what effect this has on liquidity.

6 Debtor days

This might indicate how efficient a company is at collecting debts from its customers and how much trade credit it has to allow. Generally, a company will want to minimise its debtor days.

The basic calculation for debtor days is:

$$\text{Debtor days} = \frac{\text{Debtors} \times 365}{\text{Sales turnover}}$$

In the case of CM for 2013:

$$\text{Debtor days} = \frac{250 \times 365}{700}$$

$$\text{Debtor days} = 130$$

This would not normally be considered a good sign, since 130 days is slow. However, it really depends on the business. For example, a lawn mower repair business might have debtor days of just 7, while a funeral director might consider 70 days to be normal.

Average balances are often used to calculate debtor days in a similar way to that used in stock turnover above.

An 'aged debtor listing' is helpful to show the value of debtors falling into different period categories such as 0–30 days, 31–60 days, 61–90 days and over 90 days. Most accounting software packages produce an aged debtor listing.

The poor liquidity ratio of CM is probably caused by poor debt collection and a poor stock turnover as indicated in the ratios. Certainly, if these ratios cannot be improved the company needs to look at more permanent methods of funding this type of business.

7 Fixed assets turnover ratio

Are the fixed assets being used or sweated? This ratio measures the efficiency of fixed asset usage by comparing fixed assets with sales. Benchmarking may be useful for industry comparisons.

The ratio is calculated as follows:

$$\text{Fixed assets turnover ratio} = \frac{\text{Sales turnover}}{\text{Fixed assets}}$$

In the case of CM the 2013 turnover is:

$$\text{Fixed assets turnover ratio} = \frac{700}{190}$$

Fixed assets turnover ratio = 3.7 times per year

Fixed asset turnover ratios vary a lot between different types of company and industry. A heavy industry company might expect a slower turnover than a service company. It is always best to use average balances rather than just end of year figures. When comparing with other analysts' results you need to know how they have calculated their ratios to make sure you compare like with like.

8 Gearing ratio or leverage

The gearing ratio (sometimes referred to as leverage) compares the level of a company's external borrowing with its equity (shareholders' funds). A company is highly geared when it has a high level of external borrowing compared with equity. Gearing may be expressed as a percentage as follows:

$$\text{Gearing} = \frac{\text{External loans}}{\text{Internal equity}}$$

For example, if a company has outstanding bank loans of £800,000 and shareholders' funds (called up capital and retained earnings) of £4,500,000, the gearing ratio is:

$$\text{Gearing ratio} = \frac{800,000}{4,500,000}$$

Gearing ratio = 18% (to the nearest whole number)

This ratio demonstrates a low level of gearing. However, you can expect different types of business to have different levels of gearing.

We have simply shown gearing as the ratio of loans to equity. Some analysts may show gearing in other ways, for example as the ratio of loan capital to total capital (loans + equity). And it is sometimes calculated using market values. The basic method described above demonstrates the general principle of gearing. However, when comparing gearing ratios prepared by other analysts you should always make sure that you are comparing ratios using the same method of calculation.

9 Return on capital employed ratio (ROCE)

This ratio compares profits with the capital employed to earn the profits. It is normally expressed as the percentage of profit before interest and tax (PBIT) against capital employed.

$$ROCE = \frac{PBIT}{Capital\ employed}$$

Capital employed is often defined as shareholders' funds plus term loans. There are other definitions.

For example, if a company has a PBIT of £350,000 when shareholders' funds are £600,000 and term loans are £200,000:

$$ROCE = \frac{350,000}{(600,000 + 200,000)}$$

$$ROCE = 44\% \text{ (to nearest whole number)}$$

This means that for every £1 of capital employed in the company there is a profit (before interest and tax) of 44p.

10 Return on equity (ROE)

This ratio shows the rate of return achieved by the equity investors in a company. It is normally expressed as the percentage of profit before interest and tax (PBIT) to equity (i.e. called up share capital and retained profits).

$$ROE = \frac{PBIT}{Equity}$$

In the case of CM for the year ended 2013 this would be:

$$ROE = \frac{260}{(250 + 140)}$$

$$ROE = 67\%$$

11 Earnings per share (EPS)

This is the amount of earnings attributable to one equity share. For example, if a company has paid-up capital of 100,000 ordinary shares of £7 and makes a net profit after tax of £60,000, the earnings per share are 60p per share:

$$\text{EPS} = \frac{\text{Net profit after tax}}{\text{Number of ordinary shares}}$$

$$\text{EPS} = \frac{£60,000}{100,000}$$

$$\text{EPS} = 60\text{p per share}$$

12 Price earnings ratio (PER)

The price earnings ratio compares the earnings per share (EPS) with the market price of one ordinary share.

$$\text{PER} = \frac{\text{Market price of ordinary share}}{\text{EPS}}$$

For example, if the market price of the shares is £8 and the earnings per share are 50p, the price earnings ratio is:

$$\text{PER} = \frac{£8}{50\text{p}}$$

$$\text{PER} = 16$$

The PER is important to investors because it shows the relationship between return and market price.

13 Earnings yield

The earnings yield is just another way of expressing the price earnings ratio (PER).

$$\text{Earnings yield} = \frac{\text{EPS}}{\text{Share price}} \times \frac{100}{1}$$

Using the figures above:

$$\text{Earnings yield} = \frac{50\text{p}}{£8} \times \frac{100}{1}$$

$$\text{Earnings yield} = 6.25\%$$

14 Dividend cover

This shows how many times a dividend could have been paid from earnings. The higher the number of times dividend is covered the better.

$$\text{Dividend cover} = \frac{\text{Earnings per share}}{\text{Dividend per share}}$$

For example, if a company has earnings per share of 60p and pays a dividend of 10p on each share, the dividend cover is 6 times.

$$\text{Dividend cover} = \frac{60p}{10p}$$

$$\text{Dividend cover} = 6 \text{ times}$$

15 Dividend yield

This shows the dividend return against the market value of an investment.

$$\text{Dividend yield} = \frac{\text{Dividend}}{\text{Share price}} \times \frac{100}{1}$$

For example, if a dividend of 15p is paid when the market price of a share is £6, the dividend yield is:

$$\text{Dividend yield} = \frac{15p}{£6} \times \frac{100}{1}$$

$$\text{Dividend yield} = 2.5\%$$

16 DuPont analysis

This is a method used by some analysts that enables them to focus quickly on key areas. It is not one that a practising non-financial manager will need to use, but it is described here briefly so that you have an understanding of the terms used by analysts.

DuPont, a US chemical company, created this form of analysis in the 1920s. It examines the return on equity, analysing profit margin, total asset turnover and gearing (financial leverage).

In DuPont analysis, the formula for ROE is:

ROE = Profit margin × total asset turnover × gearing factor

The formula is broken down further into:

ROE = (Net income/revenues) × (revenues/total assets) × (total assets/shareholders' equity)

For example:

Total assets	£30,000
Equity	£5,000
Revenue	£15,000
Net income	£2,000

ROE = (£2,000/£15,000) × (£15,000/£30,000) × (£30,000/£5,000) = 0.13 × 0.50 × 6 = 0.39 or 39%

A DuPont analysis uses the numbers shown in profit margin, total asset turnover and gearing/leverage to find the ROE. It shows what is driving a company's ROE and how operating efficiency/profit margin, asset turnover and leverage affect the overall ROE.

The three factors used in a DuPont analysis are broad and no substitute for a detailed analysis. However, they enable an analyst to focus on key areas of weakness.

Alternative US and IAS accounting terms are also in use – see page xi for a short list.

Action checklist

1 Understand how to calculate the ratios described in this checklist

Consider ratios under the following areas:

- liquidity
- profitability
- activity/efficiency
- capital structure.

2 Familiarise yourself with abbreviations

For example:

- COGS – cost of goods sold
- GM – gross margin
- EBIT – earnings before interest and taxation
- EBITDA – earnings before interest, taxation, depreciation and amortisation
- EPS – earnings per share
- NBIT – net profit before interest and taxation
- ROA – return on assets.

3 Monitor key business ratios

Decide which ratios are important to your business performance and monitor these daily. If you are managing an entire business, keep a constant watch on cash, gross margin and overheads. If you are a departmental manager, you should, perhaps, identify one particular ratio that is appropriate to your area of business activity and monitor this constantly.

4 Use ratio analysis to identify strengths and weaknesses compared with the competition

Consider too what return your business provides for investors compared with other investment opportunities. Identify an appropriate and manageable level of gearing and monitor this regularly.

5 Benchmark ratios

Find something useful and relevant to compare/benchmark your own ratio with/against. Remember, however, that financial ratios may not always be directly comparable (without adjustment) between companies as they may use different accounting practices. When making comparisons check that the ratios you are comparing have been calculated in the same way. Remember too that ratios are industry specific. For example, a manufacturing company that has lots of assets (machinery) will have a lower return on assets than a marketing company that has fewer assets on its balance sheet. A marketing company's main assets may be staff talent, which is not shown or measured on a balance sheet. Analyse the financial statements of your own and other companies, and compare and seek reasons for differences in ratios.

As a manager you should avoid:

- jumping to the wrong conclusions and making quick judgements
- failing to compare like with like
- forgetting to allow for seasonal and other trade variations
- spending too much time on ratios that have little impact on final results or on your area of business activity
- unnecessary complexity and spread sheet consolidation errors
- simply replacing a mass of financial data with a mass of business ratios
- assuming that year-end figures represent a normal picture of certain accounts such as stock levels.

Drawing up a budget

A budget is a statement of expected expenditure or income that has been allocated under a set of headings, for a set period of time.

Budgeting is at the heart of the way organisations measure what they want to achieve. It is a key tool in planning and integrating activities, controlling expenditure, allocating funds, indicating performance against targets and achieving strategic aims. Organisations increasingly involve additional staff, as well as accountants and finance directors, in drawing up a budget, and modern managers are generally expected to have some financial knowledge and to take some financial responsibility.

Drawing up a budget involves numerical skills as well as people skills such as negotiating and listening. It is not a mechanistic process, but a dynamic one, drawing managers throughout the organisation into considering future plans and goals within the context of the organisation's strategy and aims.

This checklist provides a basic introduction to the process of drawing up a budget for managers who may have little financial expertise, but are responsible for drawing up and presenting a budget for their area of responsibility.

Action checklist

1 Identify the organisation's key plans and objectives

Key objectives need to be identified so that you are aware of
the essential priorities to consider when preparing your budget.
Budgeting is to some extent a secondary process – secondary,
that is, to the strategic or business plans of the organisation. Only
when these are clear can a suitable budget be prepared. Should
it, for example, be a budget for growth or for maintaining the
current position? This will affect the way you draw up the figures.

2 Determine the key or limiting factors

Some key factors limit growth in all organisations. Common
examples include the volume of sales, the number of customers
and the manufacturing plant available. Whatever the key factors,
they will be significant for planning and budgeting purposes.
There is no point in drawing up a budget based on selling a
high volume of goods, for example, if this is either unrealistic or
impractical.

3 What is coming in?

Look at the range of income sources: are you generating funds,
or is money allocated at the beginning of each year? Will all the
money you have noted down really be received or will some come
in during the next financial year, or fail to materialise? How much
income is guaranteed?

4 What is going out?

Estimate your expected costs and break them down under
different headings. The range of cost headings usually include
those related to:

- staffing – for example, wages, pensions, training
- premises – for example, rent, repairs, heating
- a company's legal duties

- resources used – for example, stationery, telephone, raw materials
- any other business costs – for example, insurance, company tax.

  The general principle is to divide the budget up under whatever headings seem sensible – but, as organisations often group headings together, ensure that there is a high degree of consistency across the company. Look at last year's budget and use the same headings as a starting point.

5   Think through the fixed and variable costs

There are two types of costs:

- fixed costs – those that need to be covered, no matter how much extra work the organisation handles, such as permanent staff costs
- variable costs – those that are dependent on organisational activity levels, such as the quantities of raw materials purchased or the amount of advertising carried out.

  The company finance department should be able to help in identifying fixed and variable costs.

6   Decide how to draw up the budget

There are different theories about how to draw up a budget. Whichever method is selected, the budget should be prepared in the same format that is to be used for reporting in the coming period. In addition, an underlying list of assumptions should be prepared and documented as part of the budgeting process, as this will make it easier to explain variances when they occur.

Incremental budgeting or **resource budgeting** is based on using the previous year's figures. So if you use this method, you will base your budget on last year's figures – with, of course, an adjustment to take factors such as inflation into account. This is a quick and simple way of putting together a first draft of a budget. The main drawback is that if last year's budget was wrong, mistakes are repeated or added to. Bear in mind, too, that this is a conservative approach, based on the assumption that present objectives are right, and that there is a high degree of continuity.

If you are using an incremental approach, work out how far last year's budget reflected reality. Write down:

- the budget
- the way it actually worked – what was actually spent and received
- the variance – how far the budget was out and why.

Zero-based budgeting is used to analyse costs from the start of each year. Assess each cost according to the current position, rather than referring back to the previous year's budget. This is a fundamental approach that requires you to redefine your objectives and justify every item of expenditure.

7 Collect all the information you need to set this year's budget

Make sure that you speak to all stakeholders before drawing up the budget. This will ensure that they are able to make their contribution and that nothing has been missed. Review the organisation's objectives and targets to see if, and how, your budget needs to be adjusted or reconstructed.

Assess all external and internal factors that may have a bearing on your performance. These may include the rate of inflation, bank lending rates, a trade prospects forecast for the following year and whether you wish to stimulate the market (and therefore need to budget for the resources – money, people and necessary equipment – to do so). Budgeting for growth also means having resources available to handle the anticipated increase in levels of business, so take care not to stimulate a demand that you are unable to meet.

8 Ask some important questions

Answering the following questions will help you prepare the budget more accurately:

- Am I clear about our strategic objectives and how they affect my area of responsibility?
- Have I forecast accurately the number of people required to meet objectives?
- Are there likely to be any changes?
- Am I clear about the income levels to be expected?
- Am I clear about likely outgoings?
- Are there any factors on the horizon that might have a significant impact on the budget?

9 Draw up the budget

Keep detailed notes on why particular figures have been recorded in your budget. This may seem obvious at the time, but if you are asked to discuss the figures six months later, you may not remember how you calculated them. Build in a contingency allowance in case things go wrong, either by setting revenue targets below those forecast, in case levels of business do not meet expectations, or by limiting expenditure early in the financial year until you get a clearer picture of how well you are performing to budget.

10 Build in budget control parameters

You or your finance department will need to track income and expenditure against the budget. This may be monthly, weekly or even daily, depending on the nature of the business.

11 Present the budget

If you are asked to make a presentation on the budget to senior managers or colleagues as well as producing a written statement, make sure that you give a realistic picture (including possible downturns and problems) rather than just attempting to impress. If the budget looks too optimistic or pessimistic, say so and explain why.

As a manager you should avoid:

- drawing up a budget without involving others
- being over-optimistic
- collecting too little information for the budget.

Controlling a budget

Budgetary control is the comparing of actual costs, revenues and performance against those forecast in the set budget, and the authorising of corrective action to stay on budget.

Budgetary control is at the heart of many managers' jobs. The skills of budgetary control are increasingly valued in organisations, and the ability to control a budget is considered an important attribute for managers.

A sound system of budgetary control can provide a firm foundation for good business management. The primary objective of budgetary control is profitable spending for desired results – covering all that is required in order to maximise the profits made or the service supplied by the organisation and to manage the finances efficiently. Budgetary control works best when a company has a formalised reporting system. This should include analysis of what happened when plans were put into practice and what the organisation did or did not do to correct for any variations from the plans.

The manager's role involves ensuring that budgetary policies and decisions that have been made are implemented; that as far as possible budgets that have been set for a manager's area of responsibility are adhered to; and that any problems are identified and addressed in good time. This will help managers to monitor organisational and team performance, give them a clear idea of their department's financial position and provide information on which to base action. The mixture of skills for controlling budgets includes gathering and using information, setting up early-warning systems, taking decisions and monitoring results.

Budgets outline expectations of performance in financial terms that help managers achieve financial targets. The master budget is the group of budgets required to run an enterprise. There are generally seven types of budgets that are set up by executives or business owners and are controlled by managers:

- income/revenue budgets
- expense budgets
- profit and loss budgets
- cash budgets
- project budgets
- capital expenditure budgets
- fixed and flexible budgets.

This checklist provides guidance for all managers with budgetary responsibilities.

Action checklist

1 Understand the figures

Make sure that you understand how the figures in the budget are made up. You need to be clear about which figures you control and will be held responsible for, and which are outside your control. For instance, if staff costs are higher than expected because you sanctioned too much overtime, you may be held responsible for the overrun; but if staff costs are greater because a pay rise was higher than expected, you are unlikely to have any control over the overrun or be held responsible for it.

The minimum information requirements are:

- types and amounts of authorised expenditure
- purposes for which expenditures are to be made
- planned means of financing expenditure.

Business managers should familiarise themselves with all the accounts used by the organisation and the main accounting terms and ratios, including revenue, turnover, cost of sales, direct costs, indirect costs, overheads, fixed costs, semi-variable costs, variable costs, break-event point, profit mark-up, gross profit percentage, stock turnover ratio, return on capital employed, interest rates, retail price index and consumer confidence index. Effective control of income, expenses, profit and assets is exercised by expressing figures as ratios and percentages.

2 Speak to your accounts department

Find out what reports your accounts department can produce for you. This will save you work, provide you with accurate figures and help you to keep in touch with accounts personnel; this is important because they are usually key organisational stakeholders. Accounts departments typically have an updated chart of accounts and monthly management accounting reports, including analyses of sales and expenses under different cost centre and departmental headings, profit and loss accounts, cash flow statements, analyses of budget variances and projected management accounts for the year ahead.

3 Set up a monitoring and early-warning system

A monitoring and early-warning system will help you keep track of income and expenditure. Paper systems which record details of the costs incurred and are checked at the end of the month can work well for small budgets, but relevant software and information systems will be required for larger budgets and can be helpful for small ones.

4 Decide on the appropriate time to monitor your budget

Monitoring the budget plays an important part in controlling costs and borrowing, but it is important to make sure that the information you use as a basis for action is as timely as possible.

Choose a review period that fits in with commitments affecting your organisation or team, for example:

- weekly
- monthly
- quarterly.

It is important to get the timescale right: if you overmonitor, you will waste time; but if you undermonitor, you may not stay in control of the budget. The frequency you set will also be influenced by the financial state of the business. If it is underperforming, reviews need to be more frequent than if income is above target. It may also be helpful to take the annual spending cycle into account, restricting expenditure at the start of the year to allow for eventualities, but permitting additional expenditure later in the year, if there is money in hand, for example.

The table overleaf shows generally recommended frequencies in a manufacturing business.

Alternative US and IAS accounting terms are also in use – see page xi for a short list.

Name of report	Frequency	Purpose	Primary recipients
Sales/revenue	Weekly	Determine whether sales/revenue goals are being met	Top management and sales manager
Labour	Weekly	Control direct and indirect labour costs	Production director and production department managers
Stock/purchases	Daily	Determine efficient use of materials	Production manager
Departmental overheads	Monthly	Control overhead costs	Department manager
Selling expenses	Monthly	Control selling expenses	Sales manager
Management accounts	Monthly and quarterly	Determine whether income, profit and investment objectives are being met	Top management
Cash flow statement	Weekly	Control borrowings and determine efficiency of cash management	Top management and financial controller
Aged debtors listing	Weekly	Credit control and monitor budgeted limits of accounts	Top management, financial controller and sales manager
Aged creditors listing	Monthly	Control borrowings and monitor budgeted limits of accounts	Top management, financial controller and purchasing controller

5 Identify variances

Use the information that you collect to identify variances from your original budget, both positive and negative. A negative variance means that you have spent more than you planned, so you need to look carefully at the effect this will have on the year's performance and review your plans. A positive variance means that you have underspent.

6 Do not assume a positive variance is a good thing

Analyse any variance: find out why it is happening and what effect it will have on the year's activity. Is it a one-off payment that has not been invoiced – that is, a blip rather than a trend? Is it an unexpected drop in interest rates (and will it continue)? Have planned activities (marketing, for example) not been carried out? Have you failed to recruit a key member of staff?

7 Communicate any problems to the right people

If you uncover a problem, make sure that information about it gets to the right people. For instance, talk to:

- your boss
- your company accountant
- your team.

In many cases, people will not know there is a problem unless you tell them. You should not take any remedial action until you have communicated with everyone concerned. Remember that communication is a two-way process. For example, your team members may be able to give early warnings of problems. Discuss variances with them too, as they may possess up-to-the-minute information on why things went wrong.

8 Take action

Provide all budget holders with regular monitoring reports. Make sure that your monitoring reports show actual and/or committed expenditure and income to date, variance against budget and projected outturn. Reports need to be made available within a time period that allows for effective corrective action to be taken where necessary.

Depending on the circumstances, there are a number of options you might wish to take once the monitoring process has been completed:

- Do nothing if you anticipate that the budget will come back into line – but make sure you can provide evidence to support your assumptions, and review your monitoring period to check that your expectations are confirmed.

- Prepare a forecast, or revise an existing forecast, of what you expect the position to be compared to budget at the end of the budgeting period.

- Propose corrective action to realign the budget – for instance, cut costs, work to increase sales, or put in a bid for underspends elsewhere.

  Once you have decided what action to take, make sure that all those concerned are informed of your plans, understand them and have the opportunity to comment on them, if appropriate. Then be seen to act.

9 Keep monitoring the budget

Monitoring is a continuous process. Do not assume that because you have put one problem right, there will never be another. Continue to monitor the budget to make sure that income and expenditure stay on course, or, at least, do not get further out of control.

Make sure that the results of budgetary monitoring are fed back regularly to corporate and departmental policy and planning activities. This helps to ensure that policy objectives are achieved. Ideally, the master budget plan should be constantly monitored, rather than just the operational plan. The following elements of the master budget should be reviewed:

- budgeted retained earnings
- budgeted capital expenditures
- changes in fixed assets
- budgeted balance sheet
- cash flow statements.

10 Communicate any changes

If it has proved necessary to change forecasts, inform all the budget stakeholders – especially if they need to implement related changes. You should also keep abreast of changes in the budgetary preparation process.

As a manager you should avoid:

- acting rashly, without thinking through all the implications
- failing to involve others
- ignoring or concealing any problems – they won't go away unless action is taken
- entrusting budget holding responsibilities to staff who do not have adequate financial training and skills.

Alternative approaches to budgeting

A budget is a financial evaluation of a plan. The budget process follows the planning process. However, it is also part of the planning process, because once the financial consequences of a plan are known the plan may need to be revised.

Budgeting is an important tool for management control and an aid to strategic financial management. This checklist explains the foundations of sound budgeting and considers how budgets support and refine plans. The main types of budgets and approaches to budgeting are also outlined.

This checklist aims to provide an understanding of:

- how budgets are prepared from plans and also influence plans
- how performance against budgets is monitored
- the principal types of budget and some alternative approaches to budgeting
- which type of budgeting is appropriate for your business.

Principles of budgeting

1 An integrated planning and budgeting process

The planning and budgeting process outlined in Figure 1 shows how budgets are integrated with plans. It is an iterative process.

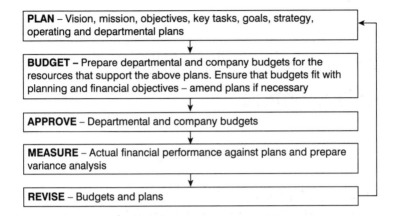

Figure 1: An integrated planning and budgeting process

2 Zero-based budgeting

If possible budgets should always be zero-based. A zero-based budget (ZBB) assumes that each year the budget holder starts from scratch and has to justify every item of expenditure to support the operational strategy, key tasks and goals.

3 Budget dependencies

Some budgets are dependent upon other budgets. For example, a budget for plant and equipment (a capital budget) may be dependent upon the requirements of production. However, the production budget may be dependent upon a sales budget. An example of a typical hierarchy of budget dependencies is shown in Figure 2.

There are no hard and fast rules to budget dependencies; each business is different. However, you have to start somewhere and the sales budget is usually the one that triggers other budgets.

As a manager it is likely that you will only be required to complete your own departmental budget. However, having an overview of the whole process will enable you to get a better understanding of your company's planning and budgeting cycle.

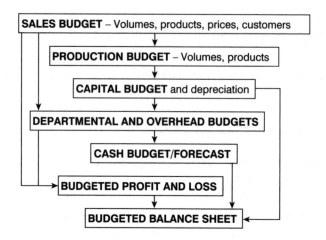

Figure 2: A typical hierarchy of budget dependencies

Monitoring performance against budgets

1 Departmental budgets

Departmental budgets for operating costs and capital equipment are what most managers have to control. Operating costs include items such as wages, rent, power, stationery, travel and other costs involved in the performance of approved departmental activities. Capital equipment costs are for fixed assets such as vehicles, equipment, furniture and other items that are used but not totally consumed within the budget period.

When preparing a budget for approval, a manager estimates what resources are needed to complete the key tasks and achieve the goals that have been agreed during the planning process. You may want to consider what was spent in the previous year to get a feel for the cost of certain items. However, you should never simply take last year's actual costs and repeat them as the current year budget, because this would not be zero-based budgeting. Repeating last year's costs will not justify a budget against approved key tasks and goals in the plan. However, few managers complete their budget without being aware of what was spent in the previous year. Looking at previous years' figures may help you to avoid missing certain items and to determine their cost.

Here is an example of a work sheet for a departmental operating budget.

Accounting department budget for 2014

Resources	2013 £'000	2014 £'000	Key task reference	Comments
Salaries	300	310	2	Inflationary pay increase 3%
National Insurance	15	16	2	Budget increase
Recruitment costs	20	5	2	Staff retention
Training	25	5	1	Reduction due to staff retention
Travel	20	5	4	Fewer trips to branches
Entertainment	1	0	2	Not required
Accounting software	1	8	2	Software upgrades/support
Stationery	5	3	2	Less paper and print
Share of overheads	17	17	2	No change
Total	404	369		

Each item in this budget has been justified by relating it back to an approved key task within the operating strategy. For example, key task number 2 could be 'to meet company legal obligations to file statutory returns'. Not all businesses use the term 'key task', but whatever term is used, the important point is to ensure that departmental expenditure is justified and linked back to an overall business plan.

Budgets are likely to be completed using an Excel spreadsheet. The above example is for one department showing the resources used. This may be termed a resource budget. Using Excel, it would be easy for the accountant to consolidate the departmental budgets showing the overall cost of resources used. The Excel spreadsheet could also pivot to show the cost of each key task. Consolidating and pivoting different views enable strategic decisions to be made.

Some departments may require additional capital equipment (fixed assets) and will prepare a capital budget. This is done on a different form from that used for operating expenditure. Capital costs for fixed assets are not consumed within a budget year. For example, a van might be used in the business for six years.

Capital budgets must support organisational goals. For example, new plant may be required for an opportunity that has been identified in the plan, or there may be an opportunity to improve efficiency. Capital expenditure is an investment that has to be justified and shown to provide the required return on investment. Capital expenditure has funding implications. Additional long-term funds will need to be found.

A typical capital budgeting process includes:

- the recognition of an opportunity
- links with corporate goals
- initial cost estimates
- the identification of financial benefits
- an evaluation, net present value, payback, etc
- the identification of alternative investments and prioritisation
- a proposal
- a decision.

The department responsible for the capital project should submit details to the finance department showing the cost, expected life, month of delivery and residual value.

2 Reporting of actual expenditure against budget

Once budgets have been approved it is necessary to report actual expenditure against budget and explain variances.

On the next page is an example of a year to date budget compared with actual expenditure report in £'000.

Resources	YTD budget	YTD actual	Total variance	Rate	Additional outlay	Timing
Salaries	260	250	10		10	
Travel	25	30	(5)	(5)		
Entertainment	15	10	5			5
Stationery	25	30	(5)		(5)	
Training	30	40	(10)	(5)	(5)	
Allocated overheads	90	90	0			
Total	**445**	**450**	**(5)**	**(10)**	**0**	**5**

Notes:

1 The total variance is (5) adverse. Actual expenditure has exceeded budget.

2 There are three possible reasons for a variance:
- rate – where there has been a change in the rate charged for an item
- additional outlay – where more items have been purchased at the same rate as budgeted
- timing – where the item is purchased in a month other than that which was budgeted.

3 YTD = year to date. For simplicity, it is often better just to consider YTD figures.

3 Variance analysis calculation

Example:

Budget: 10kg of powder @ £5 per kg   £50
Actual: 12kg of powder @ £4 per kg   £48
Total variance: £2 favourable

This is because:

Additional outlay: 2kg @ £5   £10 adverse
Rate: 12kg @ £4   £12 favourable
Total variance: £2 favourable

A timing variance would simply reflect that the powder had been purchased in an earlier or later month than budgeted.

Nearly all variances can be explained under the categories of rate, additional outlay and timing. Budget holders should get used to this discipline. It provides consistency of approach and avoids lengthy explanations that cannot be consolidated by the accountant.

Some basic budgets

Budget holders should only ever be responsible for expenditure they can control. True control can only be exercised at the point of commitment, although this can be assisted by periodic reporting of actual against budgeted expenditure.

The basic budgets in most organisations are:

- sales revenue budget
- production budget
- materials budget
- labour budget
- overheads budget
- research and development budget
- capital budget.

Sales budget

The sales budget is important because most other budgets depend upon and support the requirements of sales budgets. For example, the production budget depends on how much product is to be sold and delivered and the sales budget might be constrained by production capacity. The sales budget shows volumes and prices for each product. The volume forecast depends upon demand, the ability to compete and production capacity. Price is determined by the market. In an efficient market it is set by the interaction of supply and demand.

Avoid optimism in a sales budget, because the sales budget is the key to most other budgets. Production capacity, sales force recruitment, advertising budgets and capital budgets are examples of budgets that are dependent on the sales budget.

When preparing a sales budget check:

- the basis for the volume assumptions
- that there is production capacity to meet the forecast sales volumes

- that forecast sales fit with the company's overall plans
- that the demand is real and that there are no territorial overlaps
- that growth assumptions are real
- that the competition is fully understood
- that sales prices are realistic and achievable
- that marketing can provide the promotion required.

Once the sales budget has been approved it is passed to the production manager, who prepares a production budget.

Production volume budget

The production volume budget determines the production hours required to produce the volumes of products in the sales budget, taking into account both opening and closing stocks. The production budget helps determine the plant capacity required and capital expenditure. Plant and machinery may be identified as limiting factors in meeting production and sales volumes.

The production budget identifies the number of direct labour hours and the amount of materials required. This will feed in to the direct labour budget and the direct materials budget.

Direct labour budget

The direct labour budget takes the required labour hours identified in the production budget and calculates the cost of labour using labour rates. This budget identifies labour requirements and recruitment costs.

A labour budget is prepared for each production process. If standard costing is used, the labour rates become the standard rates used.

Direct materials budget

The direct materials budget determines how much material is required to produce the production budget volumes. Material usage is charged at cost or standard cost to give the direct materials budget.

Budgeted contribution

When the sales budget and the direct labour and direct materials budgets have been prepared, it is possible to calculate the budgeted contribution (gross margin).

For example:

2014 Budget

Sales	£1,200,000
Direct labour	(£140,000)
Direct materials	(£360,000)
Gross profit (contribution)	£700,000

Gross margin: 700,000/1,200,000 = 58%

The gross profit before any allocation of overheads is the contribution towards fixed overheads and profits. The gross margin percentage is a key 'dashboard' figure. Actual against budgeted gross margin is always closely monitored.

Overhead expenditure budget

Certain departments in a company, such as finance and marketing, are not directly involved in the manufacturing or production process. The costs of these departments do not usually vary with the level of production as direct costs do. Within a budget year they are generally considered to be either fixed or semi-fixed costs.

Sometimes the costs of one department are allocated to another department (another cost centre). This is a form of internal charging and may occur when an internal customer is identified. Internal charging works best when the internal customer has the ability to 'shop outside'. This can become complicated and confusing, and many managers and finance directors do not support this concept. However, many companies have some limited form of cost allocation from one department to another.

Research and development budget

Research and development costs are generally considered in two principal categories:

- pure research – where no particular market offering has been identified

- applied research – where a specific product has been identified.

Pure and applied research need to be budgeted separately because they have different accounting and taxation treatments. A research and development budget shows the costs of each project and differentiates between pure and applied research.

Capital budget

Capital expenditure (sometimes referred to as CAPEX) relates to items that are not fully consumed within a budget period and requires different accounting and, therefore, budgeting treatment. Examples of capital expenditure are buildings, equipment, fittings of a permanent nature, large main-frame-type computers (generally not personal computers), motor vehicles and improvements to existing assets.

Because capital expenditure is not totally consumed within the budget year it is not written off to the profit and loss account. It is shown in the balance sheet as an asset and only the portion of capital expenditure used within the year (depreciation) is written off. There are a number of ways of estimating depreciation, but it is usually calculated by dividing the asset cost, less any residual value, by the expected lifetime of the asset.

The taxation treatment of capital expenditure in the UK is usually through a system of capital allowances.

Capital expenditure requires particular board approval and sanctioning because it is an investment rather than just an operational decision. Once a capital budget has board approval, the executive responsible for the capital project is normally required to go back to the board for capital expenditure approval before a final order is placed with a supplier. The finance director must also arrange suitable long-term funds, term loan or equity.

Capital rationing

Capital is a scarce resource and it may not be possible to undertake all the capital projects in a budget. Choices may have to be made. A business will normally seek to maximise overall profits.

Projects can be ranked in terms of their net present value (NPV). The NPV is simply the total of the present values of the cash flow of a project.

The present value (PV) of a future value (FV) is:

$$PV = FV \times \frac{1}{(1+r)^n}$$

Where:

$$PV = \text{present value}$$
$$FV = \text{future value}$$
$$r = \text{compound rate of interest or discount rate}$$
$$n = \text{the period or number of years.}$$

For example, a project yields £6,000 in three years' time. The rate of inflation is 5% per year. The present value would be:

$$PV = £6,000 \times \frac{1}{(1+0.05)^3}$$

$$PV = £6,000 \times \frac{1}{1.158}$$

$$PV = £6,000 \times 0.864$$

$$PV = £5,184$$

If a business has only a limited amount of capital to invest, it will seek to maximise its return by investing in those projects that produce the highest net present value.

For example, a business has £2,000 to invest and there are three project options:

Project	Outlay (£)	NPV (£)	Return (%)
Project 1	600	300	50
Project 2	900	414	46
Project 3	700	266	38
Total	2,200	980	45

Assuming that the projects have to be completed in total or not at all, the business might select projects 1 and 2. This would produce the highest net present value:

Project	Outlay (£)	NPV (£)	Return (%)
Project 1	600	300	50
Project 2	900	414	46
Total	1,500	714	48

Investing £1,500 in projects 1 and 2 out of the £2,000 of available funds produces an NPV of £714.

Capital rationing decisions are an essential part of the budget process. They can get complicated.

Action checklist

1 Choose the right approach to budgeting

In most organisations the finance director chooses the method of budgeting to be adopted. As a manager you need to understand the method adopted.

The principal approaches to budgeting you are likely to encounter are as follows:

- **Zero-based budgeting (ZBB)** – starts with a 'blank sheet' and largely ignores what has been spent in previous years. Each item has to be justified against planned key tasks and goals.

- **Resource budgeting** – often referred to as incremental budgeting or 'last year's costs plus a bit'. For the reasons discussed above this method is not favoured, but it is still widely used.

- **Planning, budgeting, programming system (PBPS)** – budgets for programmes of activity, pivoting the resource budget against programmes. It started in the US military and is used in a variety of adapted forms.

- **Flexible budgeting** – simply allows for interim changes to the budget as explained in Figure 1 (the integrated planning and budgeting process).

- **Priority-based budgeting (PBB)** – considers priorities and scarce resources in a way similar to that described above under capital budgeting prioritisation.

Most finance directors choose a combination of ZBB and resource budgeting.

2 Allow sufficient time to produce your budget

The finance director will produce a budget timetable some months before the start of the budget period. Schedule this in and allow sufficient time to produce a meaningful budget. It is a good time to examine all your activities and costs. Expect last-minute changes as the process nears completion.

3 Link your budget to the plan

Make sure that you can link each item of expenditure back to a key task, goal or some other aspect of the plan.

4 Show your budget in two dimensions

Your budget should show the estimated cost of resources and be capable of pivoting to show the cost of each key task or goal.

5 Training and participation

Obtain training from your finance director, as necessary, and make sure that your staff participate in the budget process and share ownership of it.

6 Chopping and changing

Planning and budgeting is an iterative process. Finance directors will do their best to ensure that key budgets (such as sales) are completed and agreed before other departmental budgets are prepared. However, once figures are consolidated the executive team may require cuts and changes. This will come back down the line. You need to allow sufficient time to accommodate changes.

As a manager you should avoid:

- basing a budget on the previous year's spend alone
- allowing spreadsheets to become excessively complex and cumbersome
- forgetting to link your budgets to organisational goals and key tasks
- confusing operating expenditure with capital expenditure
- underestimating the time it takes to produce a meaningful budget
- starting your budget calculations before plans are agreed.

Introducing performance measurement

A performance measurement system is an organised means of defining measures of performance and gathering, recording and analysing information in order to monitor performance against objectives, identify areas for improvement and take action to improve performance as necessary.

A key performance indicator (KPI) is a measure against which the management of any activity can be assessed. Measurement against the indicator enables managers to assess how efficiently, effectively or cost-effectively the operation is performing.

Performance measures provide a quantitative answer to whether you are reaching or exceeding targets. The use of performance measures requires the collection of raw data and the use of a formula to convert this into a numerical unit. For example, a target may have been set to reduce the proportion of customer complaints from 10% of total sales to 5% (the indicator). A formula to determine whether this has been achieved would look like this:

$$\frac{\text{Total number of complaints}}{\text{Total number of sales}} \times 100 = \text{\% of complaints}$$

Performance measures are used to assist in tracking organisational performance against objectives. It is crucial that any system of performance measurement is fully aligned with the organisational mission, strategy and values, and that it is integrated into the overall system of performance management which sets and monitors the achievement of organisational, departmental, team and individual objectives.

To evaluate the performance of an organisation or department, credible and reliable measures need to be in place. This checklist provides some principles to help managers introduce or improve performance measurement in their organisation and considers questions such as what to measure, how to measure it, what targets to set, how to gather, record and analyse performance information and how to take action on the results.

Effective performance measurement can identify areas for improvement, help to keep performance on track, alert the organisation to potential threats and enable managers to make decisions based on reliable results rather than instinct or guesswork. The generation of meaningful and actionable data can be a powerful tool for influencing behaviour across the organisation and for keeping one step ahead of the competition. The establishment of successful performance measurement processes requires careful planning and the investment of time and resources.

Measuring performance has many advantages and enables an organisation to:

- understand the current position
- predict future financial performance
- maintain a record of historical performance
- identify strengths and weaknesses
- determine whether improvements have actually taken place
- establish a programme to benchmark against competitors, other organisations or previous results.

The financial measures traditionally used for performance accounting are now more commonly balanced with non-financial measures such as customer satisfaction and on-time delivery to gain a more rounded picture of overall performance.

Action checklist

1 Designate those responsible for the performance measurement system

This should include people drawn from all levels and departments of the organisation who will be responsible for the design, implementation, management and review of performance measures. Appoint a coordinator (someone with project management experience who commands respect and can get things done) to oversee the system.

2 Ensure the support of employees

It is fundamental that senior management fully support the system from the outset. Without their support it will be more difficult to instigate change and influence decision-making based upon the results of the measures.

It is equally important to win the support and cooperation of all other employees. Achieve this by explaining clearly why a performance measurement system is being introduced. Highlight the benefits effective performance measurement will bring, emphasising it as a positive exercise. Be prepared for a negative reaction from employees who may view it as a form of personal monitoring. Allay anxiety by communicating clearly, openly and honestly about the entire process, gaining buy-in from its inception. Provide an opportunity for employees to raise any concerns they may have.

3 Identify the activities to be measured

The selection of the right measures is crucial, as the relevance of the results depends on what is measured.

Questions that should be considered when deciding what and how to measure performance include:

- What products or services do we provide?
- Who are our customers and stakeholders (internal and external)?
- What do we do?
- How do we do it?

Think about the activities that contribute to the achievement of organisational goals and are vital for success. Resist the temptation to focus solely on measures where you know that the organisation will score highly.

The number of activities to be measured will vary, but as a guide the main areas for performance measurement typically include financial, market, environment, operations, people and adaptability. Avoid measuring too many activities for the sake of it – this will simply create an overwhelming set of results which will cause confusion and be difficult to analyse and act upon. It is helpful to place activities in order of priority to ensure that the principal drivers of success are acted upon first.

4 Establish key performance indicators

Once the activities to be measured have been defined it is necessary to identify what information is required in relation to each one. Consider what success actually looks like and decide what level of performance needs to be achieved. Consider the indicators that will best reflect the key success factors. For each of the critical activities selected for measurement, it is necessary to establish a key performance indicator (KPI).

Good performance indicators are:

- realistic – they do not require unreasonable effort to meet
- understandable – they should be expressed in simple and clear terms
- adaptable – they can be changed if conditions change
- economical – the cost of setting and administering should be low in relation to the activity covered
- legitimate – they should be in line with or exceed legislative requirements
- measurable – they should be capable of being communicated with precision.

A period of observation may be appropriate if this is the first time an indicator is to be established for an activity. Additionally, similar organisations may be prepared to offer information on the targets they set; this can then be used to establish indicators of your own. From each performance indicator you will be able to identify what data need to be collected.

5 Provide a 'balanced' set of measures

Linking measures to key success factors is critical to effective performance measurement, and introducing a balance of financial and non-financial measures offers the flexibility to achieve this. A company's success is often judged by how it performs financially. Therefore, traditional financial measures are valuable for both senior managers and external stakeholders. However, many aspects of performance, such as customer satisfaction, product quality and delivery times, cannot be captured by financial measures alone. For many employees, operational and non-financial measures are more easily aligned with personal objectives than financial measures are, which helps in gaining employee support for performance measurement. Use both forms of measurement to gain a complete picture of overall performance.

6 Collect the data

Once the measures have been decided and agreed, the next step is to determine how the data will be collected and by whom. Ask yourself:

- What am I trying to measure?
- Where will I make the measurement?
- How accurate and precise must the measurements be?
- How often do I need to take the measurement?

For activities that are undertaken frequently, it may be feasible only to measure a sample, say at every eighth event. In many cases the data required for performance measurement will already exist, for example in databases or log books. There will be instances where an automated data collection system can or should be installed to provide accurate data without the need for human intervention.

As appropriate, inform individuals when they should start collecting data and how it should be presented, for example in graphs, tables, datasheets or spreadsheet formats. All the data should be passed on to those responsible for data analysis.

7 Implement the system with care

The introduction and launch of new performance measures is a major operation. Adequate time and resources need to be planned in advance to ensure a smooth launch and to minimise disruption. Communicate the timescale for implementation widely and make sure that everyone is fully aware of its intended format and use. Carrying out a pilot or 'soft' launch will help to identify any potential problems.

8 Analyse the data

Before drawing conclusions from the data, verify that:

- the data appear to answer the questions that were originally asked
- there is no evidence of bias in the collection process
- there is enough data to draw meaningful conclusions.

Once the data have been verified the required performance measurement can be formulated. This may involve the use of a computer spreadsheet if there is a large amount of data. The results of the performance measures should be compared with the indicator set for each activity.

9 Consider whether the indicators need to be adjusted

Once the indicators have been analysed the following may be observed:

- the activity is underperforming – in this case the indicator should be left as it is, but the reasons for failure should be identified and action to remedy the situation should be taken

- variance is not significant – in this case a higher indicator should be set to achieve continuous improvement

- the indicator is easily achieved – in this case consider that continuous improvement is unlikely to be encouraged if indicators are not challenging.

Consider how to adjust the indicators in order to gather meaningful data and put the necessary amendments in place.

10 Communicate the results

Summarise the data and prepare a report by following these steps:

- categorise the data and use graphs to show trends

- make sure that the report compares the results with goals and/or standards

- ensure that all performance measurements cover the same period, starting and ending in the same month or year

- adopt a standard format by using the same size for sheets and charts

- draw basic conclusions.

Share the findings of the report widely with both employees and external stakeholders. Don't be tempted to gloss over negative results or, worse still, ignore them. Communication needs to be consistent, timely, accurate and unbiased. Only then will performance measurement become credible and useful.

Choose the most appropriate communication channel to suit the audience: email, intranet, newsletter, or a formal presentation or meeting. Consider communicating positive results to suppliers or customers too, as a means of promotion; for example, '99% of customers rate the products as excellent'. It may be beneficial to follow up the distribution of data with a workshop to ensure that everyone understands the implications of the results.

11 Take action

Identify areas for improvement and consider what steps may be needed to achieve improvements. Negative results may raise awareness of issues that may have been largely unknown or confirm what was suspected. Positive results can also be used to make further improvements. Even good practice can be improved upon, so avoid complacency and utilise the results to continue to make innovative improvements. Discuss the need for changes with relevant individuals, assign responsibility for action and monitor recommended improvements. Equip employees with the tools and resources required, and consider whether training or development activities are needed.

12 Continue to measure performance and evaluate the performance measures

The process of collecting data and analysing performance should be continuous. Goals and standards should be increased as performance improves, or adjusted as activities change. Measures will be relevant only if the activity being measured remains the same. Aim to review each set of measures annually at least to make sure that they remain relevant. Consistency in the testing and measurement of different activities will help to track performance over time.

As a manager you should avoid:

- failing to align performance measures with organisation strategy and objectives
- setting performance measures in stone – modify them as processes and activities change
- failing to act on the results of performance measurement

- underestimating the resources (staff and time) that measuring performance will consume
- introducing too many measures.

Managing working capital

Working capital refers to the current assets of the firm, i.e. cash, and those items that can be converted into cash within the next twelve months, such as stock and work-in-progress, and sums owed by debtors.

Net working capital is defined as the difference between current assets and current liabilities. Current liabilities consist of amounts that are owed by the firm that will be paid within 12 months. The major proportion of current liabilities is often, but not always, owed to trade creditors, i.e. amounts owed to suppliers and accrued expenses.

Effective management of working capital is sometimes overlooked as a critical success factor by companies struggling for competitive advantage amid fierce competition. Capital that is unnecessarily locked up weighs performance down rather than being available for investment and value creation for shareholders.

For most businesses, the control of working capital is fundamental to their finances, and good working capital management can improve their cash position – particularly in an economic downturn, where other forms of credit are not readily available. Working capital management involves the control of stock, debtors and creditors and may involve a number of employees in the process.

Implementing good working capital management will help to earn interest or reduce interest payments and it will assist in producing a realistic annual budget. Good working capital management will also help managers to take financial responsibility, think about the future and plan accordingly, and measure their own performance and the performance of their team, and it will assist managers in different parts of the organisation in coordinating their activities.

Action checklist

1 Establish systems to measure working capital

Make sure that levels of working capital can be measured accurately and regularly, ideally daily and certainly weekly. Establish systems that will allow you to state the amount of cash, debts, stock, work-in-progress and sums owed to creditors.

2 Record past and current levels of working capital

Knowing your current and past levels of working capital is a useful starting point. This helps with setting a realistic budget and will enable you to establish times of the month or year when elements of working capital are normally higher or lower. For example, some businesses hold higher levels of stock as Christmas approaches.

3 Benchmark your levels of working capital

Although it can be difficult, it is useful if you can compare your levels of working capital with similar organisations. You may also find it helpful to benchmark against companies outside your sector in order to raise your own levels of working capital above the industry norm. Some organisations may be willing to share information with you on a regular basis. At the very least you may be able to obtain their annual financial accounts and calculate useful ratios.

Stock turnover

This is the rate at which stock moves through an organisation. It is calculated by dividing the cost of sales by the average stock. For example, if the material cost of your sales was £500,000 and your average stock was worth £300,000 in a given year:

$$\frac{£500,000}{£300,000} = 1.66 \text{ times per year}$$

A higher score indicates that stock is lower and therefore less capital is tied up. This is generally better for business, although there are all sorts of variables that affect the optimal amount of stock turnover. Therefore, you will need to consider what the best level of stock turnover is for your industry or type of business.

Debtor days ratio

This shows how long, on average, your customers are taking to pay for goods. For example, your customers owe you £14,000 on a given date. Your annual sales turnover is £100,000. Multiply the amount owed by the days in the year, 365, and divide the result by the annual turnover, £100,000:

$$\frac{(£14,000 \times 365)}{£100,000} = 51 \text{ days}$$

So each customer is taking 51 days, on average, to pay. Remember this calculation can be distorted if your business is seasonal, so it works best if your invoices are spread evenly throughout the year. A lower figure is better, as cash is being received faster from customers.

Creditor days ratio

This shows how long, on average, you are taking to pay your suppliers. For example, you owe your suppliers £9,000 on a given date, and across the year you pay out £150,000. Multiply £9,000 by the days in the year, 365, and divide the result by the total amount you pay:

$$\frac{(£9,000 \times 365)}{£150,000} = 22 \text{ days}$$

Suppliers are, on average, being paid in 22 days. Again, seasonal differences can influence the results, so this calculation works best when your purchases are made evenly during the year. A higher figure is better, as cash remains in the organisation for longer. Delayed payments could cause cash flow problems to suppliers, particularly to small businesses. There is also legislation in place that gives small businesses the right to charge interest for late payments.

4 Look for improvements

There are a number of ways in which lower stocks and sums owed by debtors, and higher sums owed to creditors, can be achieved:

- stock and work-in-progress
  - forecast sales accurately
  - improve stock-control systems to identify overstocking or understocking
  - where appropriate, get suppliers onto a 'just-in-time' system (where, in effect, they hold the stock for you)
  - minimise your holdings of finished goods by accelerating the dispatch process
  - eliminate slow-moving lines
  - where appropriate, hold one central store, rather than several.

- debtors
  - agree trade terms with customers
  - carry out checks to verify that prospective customers can pay
  - establish an effective credit control system with a sensible collection policy
  - ensure that statements and invoices are issued correctly and promptly
  - offer early payment discounts and charge interest on overdue debts
  - follow up late invoices in person
  - resolve disputed invoices quickly
  - pay commission to sales people on receipt of cash from customers, rather than when the sale is agreed/invoiced.

- creditors
  - agree trade terms with suppliers or lenders, for example banks
  - delay payment to suppliers until the last day of trade terms
  - calculate whether it is worth paying suppliers early in order to qualify for discounts.
- cash
  - predict cash surpluses and make investment plans
  - predict cash shortages and make prior arrangements with banks and other lenders
  - ensure that you borrow from the cheapest source, but be aware of penalties for late payment
  - deposit cash at the bank every day if practicable.

It is likely that some improvements will lead to other costs being added elsewhere; for example, the frequent deliveries that accompany a just-in-time system may add more in transport costs than is saved through holding less stock. Therefore, careful thought about the consequences of any changes is required to make beneficial trade-off decisions.

5 Set targets and incentives

Targets and incentives can be set in each of the areas listed above. For example, a bonus could be paid for the achievement of a lower debtor days figure. Any incentives should not be limited just to the finance department. For example, the sales force is crucial here – if people are rewarded for growth alone, they may focus on the initial sale at the expense of getting a timely payment.

6 Establish and monitor cash and working capital budgets

You may need the help of an accountant to establish realistic cash and working capital budgets. These should give predictions for the levels of cash, stock, debtors and creditors on a weekly or monthly basis.

Regularly compare actual performance against budget and take appropriate action. For instance, if stock levels are higher than budget, you may need to review the list of slow-moving products and possibly discontinue some of them.

7 Foster a culture of value

Although it is unlikely that everyone in your organisation will have a thorough knowledge of working capital, key people operating at all levels throughout the company should have some awareness of it and be prepared to contribute to improving the management of working capital. If key performance indicators are devised which drive working capital performance, this enables directors to stay in the picture. At a more junior level, promote awareness of the concept of working capital, and encourage employees to make suggestions and improvements.

Effective working capital management is an important driver of a company's profitability, so it is in the interest of all employees that it is done well.

As a manager you should avoid:

- being over-optimistic
- leaving too little time for planning
- drawing up a working capital plan without involving key people, including, for example, your bank manager.

Financial forecasting

Financial forecasts are estimates of the future financial position of an organisation. They may use internal accounting, production and sales data, and external information regarding markets and the economy to predict the financial position of a company at some time in the future.

The purpose of this checklist is to explain what financial forecasts are, how they are prepared and what they are used for.

Action checklist

1 Understand the parameters of the financial forecast

Defining scope is the first stage in financial forecasting. Decide whether you are developing a financial forecast for:

- an entire economy
- an industry sector or group of organisations
- a company (a comprehensive forecast including a forecast balance sheet)
- a department, process, activity or subsidiary of a company
- a specific issue or decision.

2 Define the purpose of the forecast

A financial forecast should address a specific question. Examples of fundamental questions are:

- What will the company balance sheet look like in three years?
- What will be the return on an investment?
- How sensitive are profits to changes in variables?

3 Define the outputs required

When you have decided what high-level question the financial forecast is addressing, it is necessary to define the specific outputs required. Examples of outputs are:

- future sales
- return on capital
- net present value
- funding required
- future cost of sales
- future gross margins
- future balance sheet
- return on an investment
- a competitor's future balance sheet.

4 Define the inputs required

Once the specific outputs have been identified it is possible to define the required inputs for the financial forecast. In the case of a small company, these may be entered directly into a spreadsheet. In the case of a large organisation, they may have to be extracted from large files and databases.

Input requirements vary according to defined output, but they may include current financial data, material prices, material usage, labour rates, production times, energy consumption, customer segmentation, market prices, demand, new entrants, inflation, economic trends, rates of exchange, etc.

5 Prepare the forecast

The methods used to produce a forecast vary enormously, from a simple projection of existing figures to a thorough examination of markets and trends using quantitative mathematical techniques. The software used for forecasting also ranges from spreadsheets to expensive customised solutions that involve systems integration, data mining, data extraction, data cleansing and general business intelligence solutions. Larger and more complex organisations require more sophisticated techniques.

Preparing a single item financial forecast such as a sales forecast is relatively simple compared with a complete financial forecast that includes final accounts and possibly consolidations. This is because a complete forecast needs to work through the double-entry impact of each item forecast. For example, the full impact of a single item sales forecast when flowed through all financial accounts would affect debtors, cash, production (material purchases, labour, direct overheads), stocks, creditors, taxation and other accounts. If you are undertaking a comprehensive (whole company) financial model, make sure that the forecast accounts balance.

A basic example of a financial forecast is given below.

A company has identified the following profile for the year ahead:

Sales volume	90,000 units
Selling price	£6 per unit
Variable cost	£3 per unit
Fixed overheads	£40,000 per year
Interest rates (cost of borrowing)	7% per year
Long-term loan	£30,000

Prepare a financial forecast for the year ahead.

Step 1: Draw up an output sheet using Excel

	A	B	C	D	E	F	G
1	Output						
2			Base case	Case 1	Case 2	Case 3	Case 4
3	Sales						
4	VC						
5	GM		SUM(C3:C4)				
6	OHD						
7	PBIT		SUM(C5:C6)				
8	Int						
9	NP		SUM(C7:C8)				

VC = variable cost; GM = gross margin; OHD = overheads; PBIT = profit before interest and taxation; Int = interest; NP = net profit

The base case assumes 7% per year interest. Cases 1–4 can assume any other interest rates required to test the final output to interest rate sensitivity.

Having defined broadly the type of output required, the next step is to populate an input data sheet from which output will be derived. This can be done on the second sheet in a workbook or on the same sheet.

Step 2: Prepare an input data sheet

	A	B	C	D	E	F	G	H	I
1									
2	Input			Base case	4% int	6% int	8% int	9% int	
3	Sales V			90,000					
4	Unit SP			£6					
5	Unit VC			–£3					
6									
7									
8	OHD			–£40,000					
9	Int. rate			7%	4%	6%	8%	9%	
10	Loan			–£30,000					

	A	B	C	D	E	F	G	H	I
11									
12									
13									
14									
15	Workings								
16	Sales			D3*D4					
17	VC			D3*D5					
18	Int			D9*D10	E9*D10	F9*D10	G9*D10	H9*D10	

Sales V = sales value; Unit SP = unit sales price

Step 3: Complete the final output sheet

	A	B	C	D	E	F	G
1	Output						
2			Base case	Case 1	Case 2	Case 3	Case 4
3	Sales		£540,000				
4	VC		−£270,000				
5	GM		£270,000				
6	OHD		−£40,000				
7	PBIT		£230,000				
8	Int		−£2,100	−£1,200	−£1,800	−£2,400	−£2,700
9	NP		£227,900	£228,800	£228,200	£227,600	£227,300

This financial forecast has shown a net profit after interest of
£228,800 for Case 1. The profit does not change much with changes
in interest rates. Therefore it is not sensitive to interest rates.

Alternative US and IAS accounting terms are also in use – see
page xi for a short list.

6 Run scenarios and sensitivity analysis

Spreadsheets can be useful for sensitivity analysis. By changing
one variable value at a time it is possible to see how sensitive the
forecast is to changes in value. If, for example, in the case above,

the input value of variable cost is changed from £3 per unit to £4 per unit you will see a significant reduction in profit.

Excel is a useful tool in financial forecasting for scenario planning and sensitivity analysis. The formulae functions, macros, pivot tables and other functions in Excel enable sophisticated financial forecasts to be prepared. Formulae can be transferred from one worksheet to another. All spreadsheets should be tested for accuracy and protected by their owner.

The example above has been kept simple to demonstrate the basics of a single item (net profit) financial forecast. It is clear that a whole organisation forecast that provides a future balance sheet will be much more complex.

7 Consider using an accountant if you are not familiar with accounts

Most managers will only have to prepare single item financial forecasts for their own area of responsibility. Wherever possible use Excel and keep things simple. Avoid the use of ready-made models that may not be appropriate for your business. Building a comprehensive business model requires an understanding of accounting principles, so use a qualified accountant if this is required.

As a manager you should avoid:

- unnecessary complexity in spreadsheets
- over-engineered financial forecasting models
- making false or optimistic assumptions
- simplistic solutions found on the internet
- comprehensive financial forecasts that do not have a balance sheet.

Internal audit

There is a clear distinction between internal and external audit. The Institute of Internal Auditors (IIA) defines internal auditing as follows:

Internal auditing is an independent, objective assurance and consulting activity designed to add value and improve an organisation's operations. It helps an organisation accomplish its objectives by bringing a systematic, disciplined approach to evaluate and improve the effectiveness of risk management, control and governance processes.

Accounting scandals at the end of the 20th century undermined public confidence in business and increased pressure on companies to demonstrate to shareholders and other stakeholders that they have effective internal controls in place, and that their affairs are efficiently and responsibly governed. The collapse of companies such as Enron and WorldCom led to the introduction of new legislation such as the 2002 Sarbanes-Oxley Act in the United States, which has implications for all companies doing business there. This has raised the profile of internal audit and highlighted the role it has to play in managing risk and upholding standards of governance. The fundamental objective of internal audit is to ensure that internal controls are working effectively and that resources are being properly controlled. It is not just about financial controls, although these are of crucial importance; it also looks at the wider systems and processes within an organisation. Through its role as a key provider of assurance to management, internal audit helps to ensure that business objectives are met and that all business risks are appropriately managed.

Internal audit should be a continuous process offering many advantages. For example, it can:

- draw the attention of management to key business issues
- identify and minimise risks
- uncover weaknesses in the system of control
- detect instances of fraud or financial irregularities
- ensure regulatory compliance
- provide independent assurance that controls are operating satisfactorily and risks are being managed effectively
- make practical recommendations for improvement
- identify opportunities for improved efficiency
- give early notice of potential problems, allowing management to take action as necessary.

Over the past 20 years internal audit has developed as a profession and audits are now normally carried out by professionally qualified internal auditors. In public limited companies internal audit is directed by and reports, ultimately, to the board audit committee. It is good practice to adopt a similar arrangement in limited companies.

This checklist is designed to give managers an understanding of the factors to be considered and the processes and procedures involved in the conduct of an internal audit, whether this is carried out by a dedicated internal audit department or by an external team appointed to carry out the audit.

Action checklist

1 Define objectives and scope

It is vital to establish clear objectives for the audit, so that results can be measured against them. In most cases, an internal audit will focus on the operations of a defined business area.

The IIA identifies four main elements of internal audit:

- the reliability and integrity of financial and operational information
- the effectiveness and efficiency of operations
- the safeguarding of assets
- compliance with laws, regulations and contracts.

Depending on organisational needs, an internal audit may focus on any or all of these.

2 Decide on the approach to be used

Internal auditing encompasses a number of approaches including:

- the systems approach, which focuses on a review of systems rather than individual transactions and processes
- the risk-based approach, which aims to identify the main risks involved in organisational operations and ensure that they are effectively managed.

The choice of approach depends on the scope and objectives set for the audit.

3 Decide who is to carry out the audit

The internal audit may be carried out by a professional team from outside the organisation, a dedicated team or function within the organisation, or a combination of both.

4 Ensure support and resources

Before embarking on the audit process, it is important that those who are to be involved understand the purpose of the audit and are aware of what is required in terms of time and effort. Make sure that all staff are fully briefed on the scope and aims of the audit in order to avoid unnecessary apprehension. Emphasise that the aim is to identify areas for improvement rather than 'check up on people'.

5 Brief the audit team

It is important for the auditor to have a good understanding of the business and its strategic objectives. Ensure that all the background information required is available before the auditor is briefed.

This might include:

- strategic or business plans
- standing orders
- articles and memoranda of association
- internal procedure manuals
- risk register or equivalent
- lists of key personnel
- organisational structure chart.

Arrange a meeting to ensure that the audit team has the information it needs; do not make assumptions about the prior level of knowledge even if the audit is to be carried out by employees of the organisation.

The aim of the meeting should be to:

- ensure that the objectives of the audit are clear
- find out how these objectives will be met
- agree a timetable and a plan of action
- check whether further information is needed.

6 Plan the audit

Plans should be drawn up by the audit team, based on the scope, objectives and priorities already established for the audit, taking into consideration the depth of audit required and the resources available. The plan should specify the controls to be examined, the audit processes and activities to be carried out and a programme or schedule for the completion of each stage. A preliminary survey may be used to confirm the approach and identify sources of information.

7 Carry out the audit

A wide range of tools and techniques may be used by the audit team to examine, analyse and test the systems and controls covered by the audit. These include documentation of processes, procedures and transactions, interviews, observation and statistical analysis.

8 Evaluate the results

Once evidence has been gathered, the next stage is for the audit team to evaluate the results. The evaluation should cover issues such as how efficiently controls are working, how effectively risks are being managed, whether control objectives are being met, whether assets are safeguarded and whether value for money is being achieved. It is considered good practice for the audit team to share any issues that are identified at an early stage, rather than wait for the formal report.

9 Prepare report and recommendations

A good audit report should cover the four elements of:

- condition – what is
- criteria – what should be
- cause – why the condition exists
- effect – the negative impact or risk arising from the condition.

The report should not just point out control weaknesses but also consider how improvements can be made. Recommendations should be supported by audit evidence and communicated clearly and concisely to enable management to understand the implications and take appropriate action. It is good practice for audit teams to involve management in discussions on areas for improvement and reach joint agreements on actions to be taken. This will help to gain buy-in and ensure implementation.

10 Act on the results

If no action is taken as a result of the audit, the time and resources invested in it will be wasted. Prioritise the areas of highest risk identified in the report and draw up an action plan to tackle the issues raised. Usually, internal auditors agree a timetable for addressing issues raised with audited areas and expect to see audit points closed out. They are also likely to follow up on them at the next audit of the same business area.

11 Communicate the results

Keep everyone throughout the organisation fully informed of the results of the audit and of any changes that have been or are being made to strengthen procedures and processes. Bear in mind that in some cases documentation may need to be updated and training provided. Make sure that the wording of any recommendations does not blame particular individuals and emphasise the positive benefits of the changes.

As a manager you should avoid:

- seeing internal audit as a one-off project – it needs to be a continuous process of monitoring and introducing improvements
- failing to communicate the purpose and benefits of internal audit throughout the organisation – it may be perceived as a threat by employees who may think it is an exercise in faultfinding.

Managing financial risk

Financial risks are risks resulting from financing or financial transactions. They are the element of business risk directly associated with the choice of finance or other financial contract. Financial risks come from many sources, some of which are listed below.

Financial risk management is the process of identifying and managing financial risk. This involves identifying financial risks and implementing steps to reduce the effects of possible future financial events.

The purpose of this checklist is to provide an introduction to financial risk and how it is managed. Financial risks can come from many quarters: some arise as a direct result of management actions; others are indirect and often unexpected.

While all managers have a responsibility for value creation and protection and carry a shared responsibility for identifying financial risks early and before commitments are made, financial risk management is a specialist area of risk management that requires an understanding of financial instruments, their use to hedge and their misuse. For this reason it usually falls to the risk manager (usually the finance director) to evaluate and manage financial risks within a company's risk management policy. In the banking sector the Basel Accords cover a wide range of credit, market and other risks; if you work in a bank, you will no doubt have access to these and to your bank's risk policies. In the UK, the Financial Conduct Authority (FCA) and the Prudential

Regulation Authority (PRA) regulate the financial services industry and are responsible for prudential regulation.

It is unlikely that financial risk management processes will protect a business from all financial risks. Some risks are well hidden, external, uncontrollable and unidentified. However, financial risk management puts policies and procedures in place to mitigate the effects and uses certain financial instruments to help alleviate the risk.

Action checklist

1 Understand the sources of financial risk

There are many sources of financial risk, both direct and indirect (embedded). These need to be identified, evaluated and managed. Examples of some of the more common types of financial risk are as follows:

- **Credit risk.** This is the risk associated with allowing trade credit. A customer may default or pay late causing liquidity problems for a business.

- **Market risk.** This is the risk of losses resulting from movements in market prices. For example, the market value of investments may go down.

- **Interest rate risk.** Interest rates may fluctuate or remain relatively stable depending on the country or countries where a company operates. In the UK interest rates have been stable in recent years. However, for many decades they were extremely volatile and a major source of risk. For example, a highly geared company with much external borrowing would be hit hard if interest rates were to increase and it was on variable rates or had not hedged against increases.

- **Foreign exchange risk.** Foreign exchange rates fluctuate with underlying economic conditions, interest rates and political policies, to name but a few reasons. Businesses trading internationally will be exposed to foreign exchange risk. For example, a UK company may agree to purchase equipment from a US supplier for a certain amount of US dollars to be paid on delivery. The rate of exchange between the time the contract is signed and delivery takes place can change, creating a loss/gain on exchange.

- **Liquidity risk.** Funds available on the market might 'dry up'. Debtors might not pay on time. A company might overtrade – engage in high levels of growth without funds in place. These are some of the causes of liquidity risk.

- **Inflation risk.** Increasing supply costs that are not identified early and passed on to customers will erode margins.

2 Understand the process of risk management

Figure 3 outlines a process for financial risk management which is similar to most other risk management models.

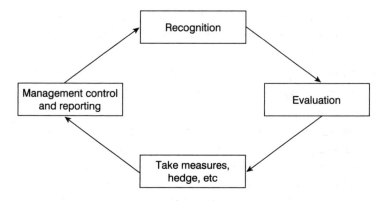

Figure 3: A financial risk management model

3 Identify financial risks

All managers have a responsibility for assisting in the identification of financial risk. They should discuss potential contracts and transactions with the company's risk manager or financial director before any commitments are made.

Look closely at contractual clauses to see how they will be affected by the types of risk outlined above. Consider also how market changes and general economic conditions will affect financial risks either directly or indirectly.

4 Evaluate financial risks

The person with responsibility for organisational risk management (in most cases this is the finance director) should run through a series of scenarios with the committing manager to determine what would happen if certain changes in variables occurred. For example, what if interest rates were to change? A sensitivity analysis can be undertaken. The usual tool for this would be Excel spreadsheets.

5 Understand the range of measures to manage and mitigate risks

Once a financial risk is identified and evaluated there are a number of actions that will limit potential damage. The principal methods are as follows:

- **Avoiding.** This is the most obvious option available but it is often forgotten. If the business does not need to take the risk because it has better alternative courses of action, avoid it all together.

- **Invoicing in domestic currency.** Ask your supplier to invoice you in your own currency. This simply hands the exposure over to your supplier.

- **Back-to-back cover and matching.** It might be possible to arrange a compensating position. For example, matching international assets and liabilities in the same country or currency, thereby eliminating or reducing exchange exposure.

- **Hedging with a forward exchange contract.** A forward exchange contract is an agreement between two parties to exchange one currency for another at a certain rate of exchange at an agreed future date. One party is usually a bank. This type of agreement can eliminate the risk of movements in exchange rates. A forward contract introduces certainty into a foreign currency transaction for a price.

- **Hedging using the money market.** Rather than buying a forward contract, simply borrow funds in the home currency on day one and use them to purchase the foreign currency required under a contract. The funds will be deposited, earning the foreign currency interest rate, and this will be more than offset, or partially offset, by the cost of borrowing the home currency funds and associated transaction fees. Compare this course of action with a forward contract.

- **Currency options.** These give the buyer the right, but not the obligation, to exchange one currency for another at a future date at a specified rate. This will, therefore, limit the downside but not the potential gains. An option can be expensive and because there is the potential for a gain, some people argue that it constitutes a form of speculation. For this reason the board would need to consider carefully whether they had authority to undertake a currency option.

- **Currency swaps.** Parties contract to swap equivalent amounts of currency for a period by exchanging debt from one currency to another.

- **Advance payments to eliminate exchange exposure.** It may be possible to settle with a foreign party in advance. This will eliminate exchange exposure and replace it with a delivery risk. It is a question of which risk is greater and what the interest cost of an advance payment will amount to.

- **Forward rate agreements (FRAs).** These fix an interest rate on future borrowing, thereby hedging risk.

6 Determine how to hedge financial risk appropriately

It is clear that there are many tools available to the financial director to manage risk. It is crucial that all managers know what authority they and other executives have to hedge or speculate and understand the difference between hedging and speculation. The most important thing is to recognise risk and manage it without any unauthorised speculation.

As a manager you should avoid:

- undertaking any unauthorised financial risk
- speculating without authority
- ignoring the difference between hedging and speculating
- being talked into complex financial transactions you don't understand.

Costing

For the purpose of this checklist cost has been defined as the amount of resources given up or consumed in exchange for, or production of, goods or services. In general it is the value (expressed in money) that has been used to produce or buy something. Costing is the process of determining cost.

When a company talks about the cost of a product it is referring to how much money or value has been used to create the product. When it talks about the price of a product it is referring to how much money it expects a customer to pay for the product. In this regard cost and price are different things.

Companies must understand how much their products and services cost so that they can determine their profitability. A clear analysis of costs will inform product sales and strategy decisions and assist with planning and control. This checklist provides an introduction to the classification of costs and looks at costing procedures.

Action checklist

1 Understand the classification of costs

Costs may be classified according to their characteristics. Commonly used characteristic classifications are as follows:

- **Fixed** – costs that do not vary within a budget period with differing levels of activity. For example, business rents are generally a fixed cost because they will not change within certain levels of production.

- **Variable** – costs that vary with the level of activity. For example, the cost of direct materials used in production will increase if production increases. Direct materials are, therefore, a variable cost.
- **Direct** – costs that can be identified directly with a product or cost centre and, therefore, allocated directly.
- **Indirect** – costs that cannot be directly identified with a particular product or cost centre and are, therefore, apportioned to cost centres or products according to a method of cost absorption.
- **Controllable** – costs that are influenced by a budget holder or other member of the management team.

As well as being classified according to their behavioural characteristics, costs may be classified by type or function. For example, departmental costs may include:

- selling and distribution
- administration
- marketing
- production
- research and development.

Revenue or operating costs are consumed within a budget period. An entirely different type of cost is capital expenditure, which relates to items that will not be consumed or used within the budget year, such as motor vehicles.

Note that the above 'types' of departmental costs may have different behavioural characteristics. For example, administration costs may include business rates, which are a fixed cost. However, production costs will include direct material and labour, which are variable costs.

The most important thing to understand in your business is which costs are fixed and which are variable.

2 Decide which method of costing is most appropriate for your business

Some commonly used costing methods are described below.

Marginal costing

This method of costing keeps variable and fixed costs separate. It shows the gross profit or contribution that a selling price less variable costs makes to a pool of fixed costs. For example:

Unit selling price	£10
Unit variable costs (direct material and labour)	£4
Unit contribution (gross profit)	£6 (60%)

Gross margin = 60% (£6/£10)

If the total fixed costs were £6,000 per year, the company would have to sell 1,000 units to break even and cover the fixed costs (£6,000/£6 = 1,000 units).

If the company sells more than 1,000 units per year, it will start to make a net profit. For example, if the company sold 1,200 units the position would be:

Total contribution (1,200 × £6)	£7,200
Fixed costs	£6,000
Net profit	£1,200

Marginal costing and contribution are used to help monitor sales activity and pricing strategies, particularly those concerning product mix.

Absorption costing and standard costing

This method of costing absorbs all costs (both variable and fixed) into product costs. The most common system of absorption costing is standard costing, which is often used in manufacturing companies. The advantage is that the full cost of a product can be identified. Unfortunately, it can be complicated and is often not understood by managers, especially when it is fully integrated into a business's financial accounts.

The fully integrated standard costing system of absorption costing sets standards for costs and measures performance against variances from standards. Standards will be set for:

- material prices
- material quantities
- labour rates
- labour times allowed
- overhead absorption rates based on the capacity of an overhead facility and the time taken to produce a unit in that facility.

Once rates have been set, entries in the accounts are recorded at standard with variance being recorded in the following variance accounts:

- material price
- material usage
- labour rate
- labour efficiency
- overhead expenditure
- overhead efficiency
- overhead volume.

Note that material and labour costs (which are variable and change directly with the level of output) and overheads (which include both fixed and semi-fixed costs and do not change directly with the level of output) are all absorbed into the product cost. Management control is exercised by monitoring the variances above.

Activity-based costing (ABC)

This is another technique that ultimately allocates indirect costs to products. ABC assigns costs to activities and then to products.

Traditional costing methods assign overhead costs to products based on average absorption rates. ABC links indirect costs to products by allocating indirect costs to activities and then to products based on their use of the activities. This technique identifies cause and effect relationships in an attempt to accurately allocate costs to products. It is most useful when indirect cost-allocation accuracy is important and when indirect costs form a large proportion of total costs.

There are four steps in the ABC process:

- Recognise and list the activities in the value chain that are related to the production process of the product.

- Estimate a total cost for each of the activities listed above.

- Compute a cost-driver rate for each activity based on an allocation method that has a direct link to the cost of the activity.

- Apply these activity costs to products using the cost-driver rate.

Activity-based costing can be a useful aid to strategic decisions concerning processes, outsourcing and selling prices. However, as with all costing systems that absorb and redirect costs, there is an element of complexity.

3 Understand how much 'contribution' each product or service makes

Remember that a product that is making a net loss under a fully absorbed costing system might still be making a contribution towards fixed costs and profits, and that the business might (although not necessarily) be worse off if it drops the product. Use marginal costing to understand how much contribution each product is making and to decide on the best product mix.

As a manager you should avoid:

- confusing cost with price – the cost of a product is determined by internal factors; the price at which a product is offered in the market is the cost plus a margin that will ultimately be determined by market forces

- getting confused by overhead absorption methods of costing, unless they are essential for the business – for example, in a manufacturing company

- making incorrect product sales or strategy decisions based on misleading product costs.

Controlling costs

A cost is the value that must be invested to acquire or achieve something. This includes investment in all activities involved in the research and development of products and services, the acquisition and processing of raw materials, and the production and delivery of goods and services.

Costs may be categorised in a number of ways, for example as fixed or variable or as direct or indirect.

- **Fixed costs** do not vary within a budgetary period with differing levels of activity. For example, business rents are generally a fixed cost because they will not change within certain levels of production.

- **Variable costs** vary with the level of activity. For example, the cost of direct materials used in production will increase if production increases. Direct materials are, therefore, a variable cost.

- **Direct costs** can be identified directly with a product or cost centre and therefore allocated directly.

- **Indirect costs** cannot be directly identified with a particular product or cost centre and are therefore apportioned to cost centres or products according to a system of cost absorption.

This checklist is intended for managers (or owners of small businesses) who wish to address the issue of cost control. In today's increasingly competitive business environment, getting the most from existing resources while ensuring costs do not escalate is one of the keys to business success or failure.

It is important to note, however, that controlling costs does not automatically equate with cutting costs or paying the lowest price, whether it be for materials, services or personnel. There will always be occasions when a period of belt-tightening is required, but frequent cost cutting can have adverse effects across the business. Product quality may be affected, thus alienating customers; and employees may become demoralised, potentially affecting both internal performance levels and external relationships with suppliers. Remember, also that cost-cutting exercises may unintentionally send inappropriate signals concerning the health of the business.

It is important to scrutinise your costs and expenses regularly – it is easier to exercise control before difficulties arise than to make corrections afterwards. Actions such as keeping financial reporting systems up to date, publishing financial targets regularly and issuing key performance measures will help managers to keep all staff informed and aware of any problem areas and establish a culture of cost awareness, which will undoubtedly benefit the business in the long run.

Cost control measures can provide essential management information, and effective cost control can help to highlight inefficient practices.

Action checklist

1 Collect data on costs incurred

To implement cost control within an organisation, it is essential to collect data on what the costs actually are and the impact each has on the performance of the organisation. Costs are often broadly categorised as labour costs and materials costs (often referred to as direct costs), and general overheads. It is usually assumed that labour costs make up the greatest percentage of total costs in service organisations, while materials costs are likely to form the highest proportion in manufacturing companies.

2 Communicate cost awareness

In successful companies, financial strategies are communicated to, shared with and owned by all employees so that they understand and are responsible for the financial implications of their activities and decisions. It is important that employees are aware of the full costs of their activities and potential alternatives to them, and understand how they can effect, or at least recommend, appropriate changes. For example, the billing of telephone and stationery may be centralised, but a true costing of all products and services should take account of this overhead on a departmental or activity basis. Where this is the case, an overhead allocation may be made to each business unit as a cost to that unit.

Where the activities of cost centres are left unattributed, the level of service use of such a centre should be considered in the cost-allocation process.

3 Examine cost-allocation processes

The budget is the keenest instrument of cost control in any organisation. More information on drawing up and controlling budgets is given in separate checklists. Budgetary control is a self-evident factor in cost control, but there are additional approaches and techniques which can support this process:

Zero-based budgeting

One method of discovering true costs is to restart the budgeting process from scratch and attempt to estimate – as if there were a blank sheet of paper – the full costs of an activity. This is called zero-based budgeting (ZBB), which works on the basis that annual budget allocations should be justified from the ground upwards. Analysing full cost allocations in this way may well prompt the question: Is this activity necessary in the first place? Remember, however, to allow for fixed costs; if an activity is eliminated, an element of fixed cost will need to be reallocated to the remaining activities.

Activity-based costing

This involves looking closely at the factors that influence an organisation's overheads and attempting to work out what constitutes the key cost factors. Activity-based costing (ABC) requires that all costs associated with a product – from research and new product development to marketing and delivery – should be identified as product costs, or split up and traced back to individual products or services. Costs that cannot be attributed to a product or service are classed as business sustaining costs – for example, finance, marketing and legal expenses.

Measuring the frequency of an activity and calculating its cost gives a model that can predict future costs at varying levels of activity. This technique is often applied to a route-to-market analysis, so as to evaluate the contribution or profitability of an individual product line.

ABC can be particularly useful where there is a limiting factor within a business process (such as machine time), as it will identify which products or processes make the greatest contribution per limiting factor and could help to prioritise or allocate resources accordingly.

Overhead value analysis

Costs are often difficult to isolate because they are made up of multiple tasks and activities which may appear unrelated in the structure of the organisation. For example, one department may receive a service from another section or department and be aware of its value, but it may be unaware of the cost attached to the service's supply. One method of tackling this is overhead value analysis, which attempts to trace and quantify the workflows – increasingly these are information workflows – which take place in the supply of services to other parts of the organisation.

Although the budget is set at the start of the year, both spending and income should be tracked as the year progresses. It is then up to management to decide what adjustments need to be made to realign the budget, and this could mean abandoning unprofitable activities.

4 Identify the various cost elements

It is most important to recognise which costs in your business are variable and will change with different levels of business activity and which costs are fixed and will not change within a certain level of activity. Some may fall in between, and these are known as semi-variable.

Major fixed and variable cost elements include:

- space, rental, local business taxes
- energy costs, such as heating and lighting, as well as the costs of waste, disposal and possible pollution – is there an environmental policy in force?
- salaries and wages – not forgetting the costs of recruitment, absenteeism, sick pay, pensions and insurance
- raw materials and services bought in – are there any agreements that could be renegotiated with suppliers? Multiple year agreements are not necessarily beneficial and even a small reduction in rates can have a big impact on costs
- travel and transport – has the use of telecommunications technologies been considered?
- general communication costs – IT systems, postage, telephone, stationery and supplies
- security and insurance – can you afford to be without them without the risk of turning a setback into a crisis? Is it worth investigating preferable services rates? Is a business continuity plan in place?
- costs of borrowing, of allowing credit and of bad debts.

Responding to adverse trends in either cost category will have very different implications in terms of any corrective action. Fixed costs are difficult to reduce in the short term; variable costs may be easier to control, but sometimes only through higher initial investment. For example, employees may be made redundant in an attempt to reduce the cost of wages, but the cost of redundancy payments will require an investment in the short term.

5 Monitor variable costs

Variable costs are normally tied to sales or production volumes. They may include:

- salaries and wages
- advertising costs
- selling expenses
- mailing expenses
- stationery supplies
- subscriptions
- utilities, such as water.

What is the continuing relationship between sales volume and costs? Is the trend healthy or unhealthy, positive or negative? One way to keep track of these costs and to analyse trends is to create appropriate performance indicators.

6 Examine your costs and expenses regularly

Recognise that effective control can help you to increase your profits on the same or even a reduced volume of sales – or of turnover. Monitor the pattern of your sales volumes over time as closely as your costs. Investigate the reasons for abnormal increases or decreases. Calculate the costs of goods sold as a percentage of net sales regularly. Look for increases or decreases in the price of purchased items, increased transport costs, wastage, or losses due to theft. Do not allow your fixed costs to blindly follow increases in sales volume which may not be repeated. Similarly, capital spending should be avoided if an increase is only temporary.

If you are using a budgeting system, remember that this will become out of date quickly; updating it with the latest forecast of performance will keep figures current and relevant. Also be sure to keep cash flow requirements in mind – this is a key factor that could have a major impact on the business. (See 'Cash flow for the small business' checklist on page 125.)

7 Analyse variances between actual and budgeted costs

A simple system to analyse variances between actual and budgeted costs each month can help you take remedial action before things get out of hand. For example, in the case of an expenditure budget, variances between actual and budget can be caused by:

- additional outlay – buying more or additional services or commodities but at the same unit rate

- rate – a variance caused when the actual rate/price is different from that budgeted

- timing – a variance caused when actual expenditure is incurred earlier or later than budgeted.

A budget holder should know the reasons for the variance. A variance analysis based on these categories will help to control costs.

Large manufacturing companies may operate a fully integrated standard costing system which sets standards for price, usage, labour/time, labour rates, overhead expenditure and capacity usage. This would support the measurement of the following variances from standard:

- material price
- material usage
- labour rate
- labour efficiency
- overhead expenditure
- overhead volume efficiency
- overhead capacity usage.

The detailed workings of an integrated standard costing system are beyond the scope of this checklist. However, it is important for all organisations to determine the causes of variances and have a method of classifying them that is easy to understand, easily managed and appropriate to the business.

At the very least, some sort of spreadsheet to monitor cost variances and the trends associated with them should be created. This must be clearly understood by everyone concerned and should be reviewed at regular intervals appropriate to the size of the business, its level of complexity and the volumes involved.

8 Be aware of how cost control affects other components of profitability

Remember that costs are only one of the factors that together influence profitability. The others are:

- sales volume/value
- net margins
- capital employed
- product mix.

A change in any of these will affect the others, favourably or unfavourably. If cost control leads to a change in costs, you should be mindful of the likely impact on sales volume, net margins, capital employed and product mix. It is not always possible to have your cake and eat it.

9 Remember quality

Remember the primacy of the customer, whose personal loyalty is to the best quality at the lowest price. Buying in the cheapest raw materials is not usually the best solution, as cheaper often means worse not better.

Schemes such as total quality management (TQM), ISO 9000 and continuous improvement programmes to improve quality in organisations have shown that it is possible to reduce costs through the systematic removal of waste, duplication and inefficiency, largely by empowering the workforce and pushing decision-making down to the level where the work is actually carried out.

As a manager you should avoid:

- forgetting that staff may have useful views on controllable costs
- not recording costs because this seems to be too difficult or irksome
- overlooking the fact that, depending on the circumstances and the way in which it is handled, cost control may have a positive or negative impact on staff morale.

Controlling credit

Allowing customers and clients to defer payment for goods and services is a common and often necessary practice. Credit control encompasses the policies, procedures and practices that ensure that the amount of credit granted and the period for which it is extended are consistent with an organisation's policy. This includes making sure that credit is granted on a systematic basis, the costs of extending credit are adequately recovered, the customer or client continues to pay within the agreed terms, and requirements for access to liquid funds are achieved. Remember the saying, 'It's not sold until it's paid for.'

This checklist deals with the control of credit allowed to customers and clients for goods and services. Credit control is a crucial component in the process of controlling cash flow. Many companies have failed in the past because management did not understand the distinction between profitability and cash flow. An otherwise profitable enterprise can fail if it runs out of readily available funds with which to meet its commitments. Failure to control credit is a frequent cause of this.

When debts are outstanding, suppliers' funds are being used to finance customers' or clients' businesses rather than their own businesses. The granting of excessive levels of credit, whether in terms of amount or duration, can also have an impact on profits, even if funds are readily available. There are many benefits in having resilient and robust systems and methods of credit control in place, including:

- the prevention of, or at least a reduction in, bad debts
- the effective control of cash flow – credit control plays a major part in this
- a contribution to improved returns on capital and net profit
- a contribution to an enterprise's ability to grow, or to survive in times of difficulty.

Action checklist

1 Assign responsibility for credit control

Make sure that a person of appropriate seniority in the organisation is ultimately responsible for negotiating, granting and supervising credit and for ensuring the prompt collection of monies due. This should be someone who has the ability to supervise the credit controller and to take responsibility if the credit position becomes questionable. The exercise of this authority, however, should not be allowed to detract from relationships between individual members of staff and their customers and clients. This is especially important in the case of specialist sales personnel who are still responsible for ensuring that sales are made and goods and services paid for in accordance with the company's terms and conditions.

2 Introduce a credit policy

Introduce a clear maximum credit policy, covering both the amount and the duration of credit. Put this put in writing so that it cannot be changed arbitrarily and make sure that it is communicated to all employees who may be involved in granting credit. Make sure that customers and clients are aware of your policies too.

When setting your policies, bear in mind the provisions of any relevant legislation designed to promote timely payment of debts. For example, in the UK, the Late Payment of Commercial Debts (Interest) Act 1998 (as amended by the Late Payment of

Commercial Debts Regulations 2002 and the Late Payment of Commercial Debts Regulations 2013) includes limits for private- and public-sector payments and provisions for businesses to charge interest on debts and reasonable debt recovery costs after specific time periods.

3 Re-examine terms of sale

Re-examine all the quotations, price lists, invoices, statements and similar documents that you issue. Do they show the terms on which you do business, especially the terms on which you grant credit? Don't be afraid of informing potential customers and clients of your terms. If you are serious about credit control, they need to know sooner rather than later. The chances are that they will respect you as a supplier that takes a businesslike approach rather than one that makes up the rules as it goes along or, worse still, has no rules in place at all. Be aware that contracts are established and that all documentation prior to invoice is amended and updated as necessary. Care needs to be taken to ensure that your credit terms are not replaced by those of a customer or client as detailed on their order document.

4 Assess credit risks

Be clear in your own mind about how credit risks for new and existing customers and clients are to be assessed, and what limits are to be set in terms of levels of indebtedness and deadlines for payment. Satisfy yourself that you and your employees handle this systematically and that the potential volume of turnover a customer or client may offer is not a factor that you take into account in setting credit limits. Recognise that sales staff are optimists by nature, especially if commission is involved. Pursue additional sources of information before increasing or establishing credit facilities for existing or potential customers or clients. These might include trade and bank references, credit agencies and rating registers, and trade and competitor sources.

5 Recheck existing customers and clients

Recheck the financial standing of all customers and clients regularly and also when a sudden substantial increase in purchases is observed. Satisfy yourself that the increase is due to successful selling rather than to a competitor ceasing to supply – perhaps because of problems in securing payment.

6 Recognise the effect of bad debts

Recognise that bad debts reduce bottom-line profits and destroy all the efforts made in reaching the much larger value of sales required to generate those profits. Bear in mind also that the existence of any bad debt means that time and effort have been expended in trying to collect the money before it is written off and that the costs of these efforts are probably 'hidden' and never identified. However, if you have no doubtful (as opposed to bad) debts, recognise that you may have been missing out on profitable business by being overcautious.

7 Review the invoicing process and the issue of monthly statements

The date on which a customer receives an invoice or statement often determines when they will make payment. Take a fresh look at the interval between the supply of goods and services and the submission of invoices. See whether the process can be speeded up – it probably can. Likewise find out how soon monthly statements go out after the last day of the month. Ask yourself, honestly, whether their preparation and dispatch is being deferred to enable some work of lesser priority to be done.

8 List overdue and total indebtedness

Prepare an aged debtors' analysis. This is a monthly list of all those whose settlement is overdue, showing debtors falling into different period categories, such as 0–30 days, 31–60 days, 61–90 days and over 90 days, and the value of debt held by them. Bear in mind that slow payment habits may reflect financial difficulties and, in this case, the whole debt may be at risk. Most accounting software packages produce an aged debtor listing.

9 Monitor the average length of credit

Calculate the average length of credit that your company is allowing, or that your customers or clients are taking. This can be calculated monthly, quarterly or even annually, but ideally a monthly figure should be produced. The only thing worse than bad news is bad news that arrives too late for remedial action to be taken.

The calculation required is: total outstanding debtor balances at month end (i.e. the amount you are owed in total) divided by sales value for the 12-month period ending at the same month end multiplied by 365 equals the average number of days' credit you are allowing.

For example:

$$\frac{\text{Total outstanding debtor balances}}{\text{Sales value for the 12-month period}} \quad \frac{£10,000}{£100,000} \times 365 = 36.5$$

So you are allowing an average 36.5 days' credit to each debtor.

Establish this calculation as a regular routine. Remember to adjust the annual sales value each time you make the calculation by deducting the sales value for the earliest month and adding the figure for the most recent month. A simple graph will show whether the average period for which you are allowing credit is increasing or decreasing (see Figure 4).

Look at the movement between the end of one month and the end of the next and at the trend revealed by the graph as a whole. This approach will highlight the length of credit being allowed or taken rather than the amount. Both time and amount are relevant to profit and to liquidity.

10 Introduce a collection procedure

If you do not have procedures and a timetable for collection, introduce them. If you do have a timetable, check whether it

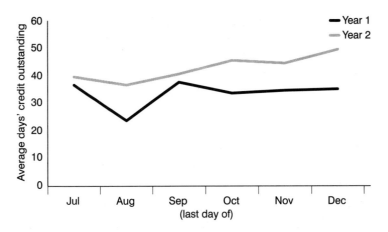

Figure 4: Average credit periods

is followed systematically. Be polite but firm in your collection routines. Always record details of any telephone calls, including dates and the names of people spoken to. Attempt to get clear commitments to dates and amounts of the payments to be made.

As a manager you should avoid:

- letting credit control dominate everything else
- allowing the volume of sales to influence your view of creditworthiness
- making excuses for bad payers – leave that to them.

  Remember also that credit control:

- is time-consuming
- may lead to difficult conversations with customers and clients who have become used to receiving uncontrolled credit
- may leave an enterprise operating below maximum capacity
- may, in extreme cases, result in fixed costs not being recovered.

Collecting debts

Debt collection is the generic name for the processes and procedures adopted by organisations to recover money owing to them after credit has been extended to customers or clients for goods and services and payments are overdue or not forthcoming.

All businesses need cash in hand to meet running expenses. The late payment or non-payment of debts can be a major source of cash flow problems, which, in extreme cases, can lead to business failure, even when the underlying business is fundamentally sound and profitable.

The implementation of effective credit management policies can help to pre-empt problems of this kind, but all companies that extend credit to customers and clients are likely, from time to time, to face situations where payment is overdue. The point at which this becomes problematic is a matter for individual businesses and may vary depending on industry or sector, but it is clear that excessive levels of debt can lead to stress for managers and financial difficulties for the business.

Debt recovery is not easy, but it is something that must be dealt with. Effective processes for following up on outstanding debts will help organisations to ensure payment of as much of the monies owing as possible and reduce the likelihood of financial difficulties. This checklist outlines sound principles for action.

Action checklist

1 Remember that prevention is better than cure

As mentioned above, effective credit management policies and procedures can help to minimise the risk of overdue payments. In addition, consider steps that may be taken to minimise the possibility of bad debts. Decide who will operate your policy. Some of the options are:

- a factoring agency
- a lawyer or agency providing access to standard stationery
- your own employees – either dedicated exclusively to debt collection, or acting as part of the accounts control or credit team.

Be aware of any relevant legislation. In the UK, for example, the Late Payment of Commercial Debts (Interest) Act 1998 and the 2002 and 2013 regulations amending it make provision for companies to charge interest on outstanding debts after a certain period of time has elapsed. The legislation is intended to deter late payment and penalise late payers.

2 Review organisational systems and procedures

There will be a need for:

- systems that detect arrears and potential bad debts early
- good communications between departments, especially sales, accounts, credit control and debt collection
- employees with appropriate specialist knowledge and good interpersonal skills
- regular reviews of policies, procedures and criteria for granting or extending credit
- firmly applied policies with regular reviews to ensure that debt collection procedures are implemented immediately when appropriate
- regular training or refresher courses in interpersonal skills, for example in developing an assertive but sympathetic manner.

3 Concentrate on big debts

Remember that 20% of your debtors probably account for 80% of the debt outstanding at any time. An even smaller percentage is involved in bad, or potentially bad, debts. Pursue the big debts first and remember that although it may be easier to collect the smaller sums that are overdue, this may not necessarily be the best approach. The effectiveness of debt collection should be assessed by the amount of money recovered and not the number of debts collected. Bear in mind, however, that:

- several smaller debts can add up to one large debt
- for a large debt a phone call before it falls due may be appropriate
- for a small debt the process may start with a letter one month after payment is due
- debts are seldom as simple as a single invoice or one month's transactions – they usually involve many transactions with invoices and credit notes over several months.

4 Write positive letters

Recognise that in the first instance an approach by letter or email is easier and cheaper than approaching your debtors by telephone. Make sure that your letters are courteous, clear and specific, and are addressed to a named executive.

Be firm, concise and unwavering. Do not include an apology, suggest a compromise or refer to the possibility of part payment. Do not avoid the issue of payment now by asking about reasons for non-payment rather than for payment. Recognise that an excuse is no substitute for your money. Understand that if you make threats, you must be prepared to carry them out, otherwise you are likely to lose credibility and are unlikely to be taken seriously in the future.

Having pursued a debt by letter or email, reapply your control of credit procedure before extending further credit. Consider putting all business on a deposit in advance or cash on delivery (COD) basis until you receive payment and the customer can meet your conditions for the granting of credit.

For maximum impact make sure that your correspondence appears to have been customised to the individual. This can be demonstrated by making specific references to the amount owed and to any previous letters, quoting dates.

Avoid using the word, 'first', as in 'first demand'. First implies 'second' or more to follow, and may give the debtor a reason to delay payment. Avoid the use of 'final' unless you mean it, and be polite, brief and firm. Give the debtor a better reason for paying than for not paying. For example:

- offer an opportunity to protect the debtor's reputation
- point out the advantages of continuing to trade together
- point out the advantages of enjoying – but not abusing – credit terms, and of ensuring their continued availability
- suggest that payment will ensure that third parties do not become involved
- express the hope that legal action can be avoided.

Many organisations have three or four letters which escalate in tone and authority. To provide proof for any potential legal proceedings, these need to be issued regardless of other courses of action.

5 Follow up letters by using the telephone if appropriate and necessary

The telephone is an essential tool in collecting payments. You should not underestimate, however, the cost and time commitment involved in telephone calls. Before calling the debtor, be fully prepared. Make sure that you have all relevant documentation to hand including copies of invoices, and that you have the following information:

- the debtor's correct name and legal status
- the name of the person you need to talk to

- the amount, date and full details of the debt
- the agreed terms and conditions of the sale or supply
- details of previous communications, if any
- the date of the last payment (if any) received
- a prepared response for excuses, requests for more time to pay and requests for acceptance of part payment.

Having contacted the right person, give your name and personalise the discussion. Recognise the need for persuasive skills to gain commitment, to convert interest into action and to find out the reasons for the delay – these may be relevant to the future generation of credit. Find out, if you can, whether a query, dispute, financial problem or oversight lies behind the delay in payment. If you are told that 'a cheque is in the post', press for details. When was the cheque sent, where from, and what were its date and number? If it was not for the full amount outstanding, why not?

If the debtor fails to honour a promise made over the phone, you need to consider what further action to take. Likewise if, after several attempts, you fail to contact the person to whom you wish to speak, escalate the debt recovery process.

6 Remember email as an alternative to a letter

Formal letters are often preferred for debt collection, but an email message can be cheaper and quicker. Bear in mind that the content may be more public within the debtor's organisation and that this may have an impact. An email can be sent direct to the desk of the recipient and therefore gain immediate attention.

7 If all else fails, consider visiting the debtor

Visiting is the least cost-effective method of collection; it is difficult for those who wish to avoid confrontation, and you may feel that you have lost face if you leave without a cheque in your hand. If you decide to visit the debtor, arrive unexpectedly, be firm, courteous and unwavering, and, if you are not able to collect a cheque, move quickly to the next stage.

8 Appoint a debt collection agency

If you decide to use a debt collection agency, use only those that are licensed (by the Office of Fair Trading in the UK) and have a good reputation. Do not pay the agency up front or agree to a flat fee. Agree to pay only a percentage of what the agency recovers. Obtain a banker's reference and talk to other users of the agency. Make sure that you know the agency's terms and conditions and that these are acceptable to you.

9 Think carefully before you instruct solicitors or become involved in litigation

Remember that solicitors are expensive and require payment whether or not they achieve results – seek advice and a price before making any commitments. Litigation is even more expensive. Before starting proceedings, make sure that the debtor has money with which to pay, you have reasonable evidence of the existence of the debt and the debt is less than six years old. Make sure that you have the full name and address and legal status of the debtor.

10 Do not return a post-dated cheque without thought

A post-dated cheque is better than no cheque. It may be paid if presented. It provides proof of debt if the bank does not pay the cheque. Consider carefully, however, whether you want to continue trading on the basis of post-dated cheques.

11 Beware of taking any unreasonable or illegal actions

Be aware of the dangers of being charged with harassment, for example by threatening violence, damaging property or breaking and entering. Know that you must not make such strong or frequent demands of your debtors as to cause them or their families concern, distress or humiliation. Also, remember that you must not represent yourself as having some official capacity with authority to enforce payment. Make sure that you are aware of the provisions of any relevant legislation, such as the Administration of Justice Act 1970 in the UK.

As a manager you should avoid:

- failing to take action to address the issue of outstanding debts
- starting by offering compromise
- forgetting that it's your money you are chasing – not theirs.

Spotting fraud

The Audit Commission's definition of fraud is:

The intentional distortion of financial statements or other records by persons internal or external to the organisation which is carried out to conceal the misappropriation of assets or otherwise for gain.

Fraud is not limited to the misappropriation of funds. It also includes the theft of stock or equipment or other assets, as well as, for example, false claims for payment for goods or services not delivered.

The focus of this checklist is on how an organisation, whether in the private or public sector, can put simple measures in place to prevent fraud. It is important to recognise that everyone has a role in spotting and preventing fraud.

Fraud is a crime and there are many obvious advantages to spotting fraud. These include:

- saving money – in the UK the National Fraud Authority has estimated fraud losses in 2012 of £45.5 billion in the private sector alone
- avoiding damage to morale – no one wants to work for an organisation where fraud is rife and never investigated
- accountability – tackling fraud is one aspect of public, shareholder and stakeholder accountability.

In extreme cases, fraud results in the collapse of companies, leading to substantial job losses, zero-value shares, pension shortfalls, imprisonment and extreme embarrassment. If fraud is not tackled appropriately, it can seriously damage an organisation's reputation and can affect the confidence of its funders, shareholders, customers and service users.

Fraud must be taken seriously. Systems and procedures to deal with fraud should be put in place and company boards and senior managers must reinforce anti-fraud messages by demonstrating their commitment to the elimination of questionable practices. The findings of Ernst and Young's latest Global Fraud Survey, published in 2013, suggest that companies are still failing to do enough to prevent bribery and corruption. Particular concern was expressed regarding a general lack of anti-fraud training, failure to penalise breaches of standards and the willingness of financial managers to justify questionable actions in times of economic difficulty.

It is not only employees that attempt fraud. It can also be committed by external third parties acting independently, for example by submitting invoices for bogus goods or services.

There are two elements to tackling fraud:

- putting systems in place
- developing an anti-fraud culture.

Action checklist: putting systems in place

1 Write a fraud strategy statement

Write guidelines to help answer questions such as:

- When does pilfering become fraud and hospitality or perks become corruption?
- Can employees accept any gifts?

Without guiding principles, it is difficult for people to differentiate between accepted custom and practice and what is not acceptable. So set out a strategy on financial integrity.

Try to develop a separate procedure that spells out clearly:

- who is responsible for dealing with fraud
- the stages involved in raising and dealing with a concern.

2 Set up an audit committee

Larger companies should establish an audit committee. This can be a useful way of setting the framework for fraud control. The committee should consist of senior stakeholders from a range of different departments (people who have insight into the causes of fraud and sufficient influence to make any recommended changes stick) and committee members (if your organisation has a committee).

It is recommended that smaller organisations seek professional advice.

The job of an audit committee is to:

- help to design fraud prevention measures and develop a more effective fraud prevention system
- review the organisation's anti-fraud strategy
- help to investigate examples of malpractice and suggest action when they are uncovered.

The audit committee can act as a reporting line for an organisation's internal auditor. It acts as a guiding and controlling influence, a policy and strategy forum, and a vehicle for accountability.

3 Tighten up anti-fraud procedures

Poorly documented procedures contribute to fraud. Make sure that procedures are clearly set out and that they are communicated and accessible to all employees.

4 Make the most of information technology

Organisations often hold large amounts of information, particularly financial information. Fraudsters often perpetrate their crimes because one department does not know what the others are doing, and this may give them the chance to carry out multiple fraud. Integrated and relational databases enable organisations to cross-reference information, both internally and with other organisations. Use information technology to share information and spot fraud at its source. Many local authorities, for example, share information about people who claim multiple housing benefits. This has proved a highly effective weapon against fraudsters.

5 Establish procedures for an effective fraud investigation

The following is based on good practice guidance for effective fraud investigation:

- appoint a steering officer for the investigation
- agree the target dates and key issues
- hold steering meetings to discuss progress, agree variations and identify future targets
- identify the actions required
- consider the likely outcomes, i.e. internal disciplinary action or prosecution
- if the indications appear serious, contact the police at an early stage and get their advice.

Action checklist: developing an anti-fraud culture

Creating the right environment to tackle fraud requires a range of initiatives, some of which are difficult to evaluate but important nonetheless. In many organisations there is a good deal of apparently trivial fraud which is accepted as the norm. Changing this perception, and changing this practice, can be difficult, and may cause some resentment.

1 Maintain internal checks and the separation of duties

The organisation should have in place a system of internal checks whereby more than one person is responsible for recording a transaction and approving a disbursement of funds or any other activity (both purchases and sales) that can affect the value of the organisation. For example, the person authorising the payment of an invoice should not be the one who signs the cheque. Have more than one cheque signatory. Have one person preparing BACS/CHAPS payments and another signing them off. These are examples of internal checks that should be part of an organisation's internal controls system. Auditors, both internal and external, should be expected to examine the adequacy of these internal controls.

2 Ensure that managers provide leadership

Any initiative aimed at openness is only as good as its leaders. Employees may be cynical about any new approach. They may have had experience of concerns being brushed under the carpet in the past. The message about fraud and corruption needs to come clearly from the top and be reinforced with action.

3 Make communication work

Involve your employees and listen to their sense of what is right and what is wrong. Explain what fraud is and the effect it has on their jobs and the services they provide to their customers (both internal and external).

- Be clear about how seriously you treat the problem.
- If it is fraud, call it fraud when you discover it.
- Use seminars, newsletters and briefing sessions to explain your commitment to tackling fraud and to report on your successes.

4 Offer anti-fraud training

Any new system needs to be reinforced with training. You can use training to stress your messages about fraud and the need for vigilance and openness and to explain the way the system works. More importantly, training can also help to instil new coaching and counselling skills that managers will need to handle concerns effectively.

5 Introduce a process for whistleblowing

It is important to open up routes through which concerns about fraud can be channelled. All employees need another option for raising concerns in addition to their line managers. This could be the chief executive or finance officer, an employee in internal audit, or a named senior manager in a larger business. Employees should feel able to raise their concerns, in strict confidence, without recrimination.

A final word

The measures listed above are suggestions. You may already do many of the things mentioned. The key is to keep a balance between procedures and guidelines and work at developing a culture of openness where feedback can be given freely.

As a manager you should avoid:

- brushing fraud under the carpet
- being soft on fraud
- ignoring the concerns of employees – they are the ones who are most likely to spot fraud.

Cash flow for the small business

In accounting, cash flow refers to the amounts of cash being received and spent by a business over a defined period of time, sometimes tied to a specific project. Measurement of cash flow can be used to evaluate the state or performance of a business or project.

Cash flow is often referred to as the lifeblood of an organisation. With it, operations can proceed smoothly, allowing the best possible decisions to be made, without concerns about the company's ability to pay bills. Without it, decisions are often hampered by the inability to pay and thus a company can end up implementing a plan or taking a course of action that is not in its best interests. This checklist is designed to help you develop an understanding of and control cash flow in your business.

Controlling cash flow means that you know where your cash is tied up. You should be able to spot potential bottlenecks and act to lessen their impact. You should also be able to reduce your dependence on bank lending, which will result in savings on interest charges. Most importantly, you should have control of your business and therefore be able to make informed decisions.

It is important for cash to flow effectively through the system (see Figure 5). Too little cash, or indeed any factors impeding a smooth and continuous flow of cash, will create problems. Without an adequate flow of cash, a company may be trading profitably in the shorter term, but may nevertheless collapse. Poor management of cash flow is said to be the most common reason for the failure of small firms.

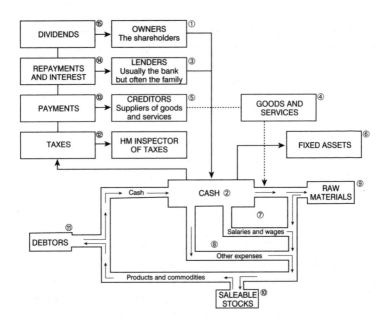

Figure 5: The flow of cash through a business

Figure 5 illustrates the flow of cash through a business. It starts at (1) when the would-be owners of the business (or shareholder(s) if it is to be a limited company) invest funds, which go into the pool of cash (2).

This investment may not be a once and for all step. There may be subsequent investments for a variety of reasons, some of which could well be positive – for example, business expansion. Others may be negative, such as a shortage of liquid funds. At the same time, or again later, lenders (3) may also put funds into the cash pool. The lenders may be the company's bankers or, in some cases, members of the family or friends of the owners of the business.

To enable the firm to start trading, we will assume that it obtains goods and services (4) on credit from suppliers (5) who become creditors. Consideration will also be given to obtaining fixed assets (6). These may range from freehold buildings to office equipment. You will recognise that if acquisition is based on purchase, and if relevant assets are truly fixed, some liquid capital has been immobilised immediately. Cash also flows out of the 'pool' in the form of salaries and wages (7) and other expenses (8), which may include, for example, stationery and additional computer software.

If the new firm is to manufacture, it will require raw materials (9) – another outflow of cash (sooner, if the materials are paid for immediately, and not much later if they are purchased on credit). The expenditure on wages and other expenses (for example tools), together with the use of some of the raw materials (7), (8) and (9), will lead to the creation of saleable stocks (10). If the firm does not manufacture products for sale, it will purchase saleable stocks for resale. The stocks will join 'the stream' on their sale and will probably be sold on credit to customers who become debtors (11). They will owe the firm the price of goods or services supplied until they pay. When they do pay, cash will continue to flow back into the cash pool (2).

Yet the cycle is still not complete. At the appropriate time, cash will be moved from the pool to pay taxes (12), to make payments to creditors (13), to make repayments of capital and payments of interest to lenders (14), and to make payments of dividends or other forms of reward to the owners, the original investors (15). The flow of cash through the business is never ending. If there is a blockage at any point – for example, if sufficient money to purchase raw materials is unavailable – it may be difficult for the company to continue operating, even when the business is healthy in every other respect. Without an injection of cash, trading will cease and the firm will be wound up.

Action checklist

1 Identify the potential cash bottlenecks through your company

A careful examination of Figure 5 may suggest bottlenecks at these points:

- fixed assets (6)
- raw materials (9)
- saleable stocks (10)
- debtors (11).

Examine these bottlenecks in turn, and consider how you would deal with any issues that may arise as a result of them.

2 Reconsider your investment in fixed assets

- Is cash unnecessarily tied up in fixed assets?
- Is it tied up in assets that are not used or could be disposed of?
- Is it tied up in necessary assets that could be replaced by leasing?
- Is it tied up in assets that represent a greater than necessary investment, which could be replaced by something more modest?
- Has cash been invested in fixed assets for reasons of prestige rather than of profit?

3 Reconsider your investment in raw materials

- Have you tied up cash in raw materials to take advantage of special terms offered by suppliers?
- Do you have an efficient supply chain?
- Are you sure that the advantages outweigh the costs of holding stocks which may not be used immediately?

The advantages must be weighed against the following factors:

- the cost of borrowing money to finance stockholding

- the loss of alternative uses for the capital employed
- the costs of physical storage
- risks of stock shrinkage.

Likewise reconsider your investment in saleable stocks.

4 Reconsider your system of stock control

An appropriate system of stock control does not necessarily presuppose precise stock records for every line held in stock. The types of records adopted will depend on common sense. The cost of the system must be weighed against a financial evaluation of the problems that the system is intended to help solve.

Some form of control is necessary to guard against theft, obsolescence, spoilage, running out of or having too much stock, or having unbalanced stock, any of which can penalise a business severely. The basic requirements of a stock-control system may be summarised as:

- a forecast of what you expect to sell and when
- a knowledge of your present stocks, updated at regular intervals
- a record of supplies received and deliveries made which should be periodically reconciled with present stocks (this reconciliation need not be of everything but only of selected items in sequence)
- predetermined and regularly reviewed reorder levels and quantities
- a knowledge of price trends, quantity discounts and the time that will elapse between the placing of an order and delivery.

Check stock at least once a year. Have you considered a perpetual inventory system or a cyclical stocktaking procedure using employees as and when fluctuating workloads make this possible? Are your stocks neatly stored in a way that makes stocktaking easy and eliminates the risk of contamination, obsolescence and damage?

5 Look carefully at your systems for granting and controlling credit

There is a direct relationship between the amount and duration of credit allowed and the return on capital and net profit a firm can make. It is assumed that in most cases it is more important to obtain the quickest possible turnover of capital rather than producing an additional return on capital 'lent' to a customer. Make sure that your policy:

- recovers the cost of extending credit
- gives the customer the greatest continuing incentive to pay promptly.

6 Consider carefully these self-testing questions on credit management

You may wish to consider these points in order to manage credit in your business more effectively, therefore allowing cash to flow more freely.

Policy

- Is there one person in your firm who is ultimately responsible for supervising credit and for ensuring the prompt collection of monies due, and is accountable if the credit position gets out of hand? The exercise of their authority should not detract from the individual salesperson's relationship with the customer, or from the individual salesperson's responsibility for seeing that the sales they make are paid for in accordance with the firm's credit terms.

- Do you have a clear maximum credit policy? Is it written down? Is it known to all members of your sales team? Are they instructed to ensure that all your customers are familiar with your policy?

- Are you clear in your own mind as to how you assess credit risks and how you are to impose normal limits – in terms of both total indebtedness for each customer's open account (including cheques in course of collection) and time?

Bad debts

Do you recognise that:

- assuming you make 1.5% net sales, a loss of £1,500 in bad debts nullifies the net profit on £100,000 sales and destroys all the effort involved in making those sales?

- an avoidable loss of £1,500 in bad debts means that a lot of effort will have been expended in trying to collect this money before it is written off – and that the cost of this effort is probably 'hidden' and never identified?

- conversely, the absence of any doubtful – as opposed to bad – debts probably means that you have been missing out on business by being overcautious?

Granting or extending credit

- Do you methodically check the financial standing of all new customers before executing the first order?

- Do you recheck the financial standing of existing customers whose purchases have recently shown a substantial increase?

- Do you use the telephone when checking trade references? Suppliers will often tell you over the phone what they would not put in writing.

- Do you recognise that sales people are by nature optimists? Do you therefore rely on other sources of information before establishing (or increasing) credit facilities for customers?

Credit control and collection

- How soon do your invoices go out after the goods are dispatched? Can this be speeded up?

- How soon do monthly statements go out following the last day of the month? Can this be speeded up?

- Are the terms of sale clearly and precisely shown on all quotations, price lists, invoices and statements?

- What is the actual average length of credit you are giving, or your customers are taking? What length of credit do you allow?

- Do you prepare monthly lists of all customers whose settlement is overdue, and do you list the total indebtedness of slow customers as well as the overdue amount? If their slow-paying habits reflect financial difficulties, the whole debt may be at risk.

- Do you have a collection procedure timetable? Do you stick to it?

- Are you politely firm but insistent in your collection routine?

- Do you watch the ratio of total debt on balances in the sales ledger at the end of each month in relation to the sales of the immediately preceding 12 months? Is the position improving, deteriorating, or static? Why?

- Do your salespeople recognise that 'it's not sold until it's paid for'? Could you consider linking part of the salesperson's commission to receipt of payments from your customer?

- Have you considered offering an early settlement discount to your customers to encourage them to pay early? This could boost cash flow for a relatively low cost.

- If you are experiencing cash flow difficulties, have you considered redeploying staff from sales to work on credit control?

Paying your suppliers

- Have you negotiated the best possible payment terms with your suppliers? Extending the time you have to pay is another way of easing cash flow concerns.

- Will your suppliers consider extending a credit facility to you rather than you having to pay for goods on order or delivery?

As a manager you should avoid:

- assuming that all sales are equal

- disregarding the customer-service department which can enhance cash flow

- mismanaging quality control.

Valuing a business

The fair market value of a business is an estimate of its value based on what a knowledgeable, willing and unpressured buyer would pay to a knowledgeable, willing and unpressured seller.

The true value of anything is the price at which a seller will sell and a buyer will buy. However, in some cases it may be necessary to value something before an actual exchange of property for money takes place. In these circumstances, it is therefore necessary to make an estimate of fair valuation.

Writers on economics have devoted a lot of time to examining the bases of supply and demand, the main elements that determine price and value. Although these theories are of great interest, and undoubtedly underpin much of what will be discussed here, this checklist takes a more pragmatic and practical approach to the subject and outlines a number of methods that are commonly used to value businesses.

In many cases sentiment may influence market-based valuations far more than the underlying fundamentals. However, at times of recession, market values may become more closely related to fundamental valuations. Most valuers use a mixture of income, asset and market information to support their estimates.

Action checklist

1 Understand how businesses create value

It is worth considering how a business creates value in the first place. Many factors affect the growth or diminution in the value of a business. Some of these are controllable or semi-controllable and others are not. A business would expect to have some influence on and control over internal factors but less or little influence over external factors. A business that is highly sensitive to external factors carries more uncontrollable risk and will find it harder to ensure a controlled increase in its valuation.

The internal and external factors that affect a business valuation can be classified as follows:

Internal factors

- quality of staff and executive team
- quality of services and products
- resources employed
- customer perception and loyalty
- efficiency and profitability
- dividend policy
- financial strength
- building of brand awareness
- agility and responsiveness.

External factors

- the general state of the economy and macro issues
- political and socio-economic environment
- interest rates
- the supply chain
- labour supply
- direct and indirect competition

- sector and industry events
- the world economy and foreign exchange rates
- brand acceptance
- environmental events.

These are just some examples of factors that affect growth in value. You will be able to identify others relating to your own business.

Because business values are sensitive to all these factors, a business must identify which internal factors it needs to optimise and how it can position itself in such a way as to minimise its exposure to the less controllable external factors. For example, a company might decide to develop a strong USP (unique selling proposition) in order to reduce its exposure to competition.

When a business has established which factors most affect its value, it should develop a strategy and a plan for maximising profits that take them into account. For example, it might carry out a strategic value analysis. This is the systematic measurement of each part of a business to establish how it might add value to the business as a whole. This will include an examination of core business activities and a comparison with external providers of similar services.

A business will want to develop a target for its own valuation at a future point in time to help it focus on and evaluate business plans. This is particularly important if there is the intention of a future sale or flotation, or the owners require an exit strategy. It is important to understand how a business will be valued, who will value it, and why they should value it. For example, a quoted company may be valued by the markets with particular attention to its price/earnings ratio. However, the company may have other valuable attributes that are not so easily measured by the market and these could affect its future earnings and real value. Business values are linked to a network of internal and external relationships. Value is created as a result of the collaboration between parts of the network. Internal company controls and processes help create value, and so does an understanding of the value chain and key external relationships.

2 Understand the reasons for and context of the valuation

A business will have different values for different buyers. The value will depend on how the buyer intends to use the business being acquired and on the return it will obtain from the business – and this may be different from the value placed on a business when it is being wound up. Buyers and sellers use the economic value of a business to determine the price at which they are prepared to buy or sell it. This is necessary for all mergers and acquisitions. Business valuations are also used for estate, taxation and a number of other legal purposes. So before a valuation can be undertaken, it is necessary to understand the reasons for the valuation – scrap value is generally worth less than going concern value.

If known, a value may take account of the price a willing buyer and a willing seller have agreed to. This would be called the fair market value (FMV). However, the market conditions during this exchange might not have been perfect. Because markets are rarely perfect, a valuation usually starts with a contextual evaluation of the economic and industry conditions surrounding the business. For example, is it a buoyant market or is it a market in recession? For a more accurate valuation, an analysis of the business's financial performance and strength should be compared with those in the rest of the industry. Competitor valuations should also be considered.

Approaches to an initial business valuation include:

- asset valuations as a going concern
- income/earnings valuations as a going concern
- break-up asset valuations
- market valuations as a going concern.

The method used will depend upon the use the buyer has for the business, and each of these approaches will relate to a particular reason for selling or buying. It is common for a business to be valued on several bases and the differences between the resulting valuations explained.

To help decide which valuation method to use, consider the reason for the valuation. Some typical reasons are to:

- help a banker when considering a loan application
- enable the taxation authorities or other agencies to value an estate
- provide a comparison with the offer price of a takeover bid
- provide a comparison with the current share price
- use as an initial guide to business value when a company goes into liquidation
- provide a valuation when planning to dispose of a significant number of shares that might give a buyer a controlling interest
- determine an issue price for shares when going public
- assist transactions when companies merge
- provide a basis for negotiations in the case of management buy-outs
- provide periodic valuations under the terms of a loan
- assist business exchange and ownership transfers
- indicate to prospective buyers the price they might be required to pay for a business
- help resolve disputes relating to estates, taxation and general litigation
- help estimate the potential effects of a disaster on all or part of a business
- determine buy-in prices for new partners.

3 Be aware of common methods used for business valuations

- **Net book value.** The value of an owner's equity as recorded in the accounts. It may be a starting point but, unfortunately, accounting records may not reflect the value of assets and liabilities to a potential buyer. For example, generally accepted accounting principles (GAAP) require that stocks are valued at the lower of cost or net realisable value. The good reason for this is conservatism. However, at the point of a business sale, stocks may be worth a lot more or a lot less than recorded in the accounts. It all depends on what value the buyer can derive from the stocks. A buyer may have access to markets through which the stocks could be converted into cash at a higher price than is recorded in the accounts. Book values may be of limited use, but they are rarely ignored and do at least provide a starting point.

- **Tangible book value.** A method that removes intangible values from the book value. It simply values tangible assets and places no value on goodwill or other intangibles.

- **Economic book value.** A revaluation of the book value at market rates. It takes account of all assets, including goodwill, and values them at the market rate.

- **Net present value of future earnings.** Estimated and projected future earnings are discounted using an appropriate discount rate to give their net present value (NPV).

- **Income capitalisation method.** Uses a capitalisation rate, which is the rate of return required by buyers for the business risk involved. The earnings are then divided using this rate.

- **Dividend capitalisation.** Considers a company's dividend paying capacity based on its net income and cash flow. Put simply, this is how much dividend it will be able to pay a potential buyer.

Alternative US and IAS accounting terms are also in use – see page xi for a short list.

- **Price/earning multiple.** Considers the market price of a company's shares divided by its earnings per share multiplied by the net income.

- **Benchmarking of sales and profit valuations.** The sales and profit multiples of a company may be benchmarked in an industry and used for comparative valuation purposes.

- **Realisable value.** Commonly used when a company is being broken up. The net realisable value of assets in a sale or auction is estimated and aggregated to provide a valuation.

- **Replacement value.** Estimates the replacement value of an entire business. It considers how much it would cost a buyer to set up a similar business.

A company may set a target for a future business value as a strategic goal. This is commonly expressed in earnings or dividend targets. Owners of a business may also wish to set a future valuation goal as part of their exit strategy. Each of the above methods has its merits and the one chosen will depend largely on the use a potential buyer has for the company. It is a worthwhile exercise to use several of the above methods to value your own company. You will probably arrive at very different valuations. This may determine the type of buyer you should seek when selling your company. The markets, on the whole, take a narrow view of company value using fewer indicators for comparative purposes. Sometimes there will be 'hidden gold' in a company not indicated by its market valuation.

4 Choose a suitable person to value the business

Business valuers need to have an understanding of the industry sector of the business they are valuing. They also need to be competent in each of the disciplines required in the valuation methods. This is why a valuer is likely to be an accountant, a lawyer or a senior banker who has been involved in the sector. When selecting a professional valuer, examine their qualifications and previous client assignments. Do they have the skills to understand the business being sold and type of potential buyer?

5 Gather the information needed for the valuation

The information required by a valuer is extensive and will include:

- audited financial statements for the most recent and past years
- interim financial statements
- financial projections including underlying assumptions for income and costs
- current sales orders and signed contracts
- supplier contracts and relationships
- aged debtors listings and bad debt provisions
- aged creditors listings
- cash flow statements, forecasts and source/application of funds statements
- outstanding debts not yet invoiced and accruals
- payments in advance/prepayments
- stock valuation methods (material, labour and overhead absorption)
- valuations for raw materials, work-in-progress and finished goods
- stocktaking procedures
- estimates for stock obsolescence
- property valuation certificates or market estimates
- property titles
- property and land surveys
- rental/lease agreements
- loan and repayment schedules
- lists of investments and securities with supporting documentation
- financial institution/bank statements
- company cash book
- cash book to bank reconciliations

- payroll details, staff, rates, PAYE and NI
- employment contracts for all staff
- directors' earnings
- directors' and employees' interests
- company organisation chart
- schedule of legal charges over assets
- debenture documents
- list of shareholders and their holdings of each type of share
- specific industry and competitor information.

This list is not exhaustive. A business valuer may require some or all of the above information and may recruit the help of others with specific qualifications and experience in certain areas.

6 Decide on the most appropriate method of valuation

As already discussed, real values are only determined on the actual sale of a business. Since valuations are always made without the benefit of a realised selling price, they are just estimates based upon a number of assumptions, not least the value to different buyers. Some of the valuation methods already mentioned are described here in more detail and their appropriateness under different circumstances considered.

Asset-based valuations and 'floor values'

Asset-based valuations may provide a starting point and a fundamental base that can be used to question the results obtained from other methods of valuation. They are sometimes referred to as floor values because they provide a base or bottom-line value. Asset-based valuations first need to consider the premise or reason for the valuation. This is best described in an example.

Universally accepted accounting practice requires that a business's stock should be recorded in the accounts at the lower of cost or net realisable value. However, in a business valuation should the stock be valued at book value, replacement value, realisable value or scrap value?

The stock valuation method used will depend upon the intentions of the buyer of the business. Does the buyer want to continue with the business as a going concern or does it intend to simply drop the stock line and sell it off as scrap? The value of the stocks within a business valuation will depend upon the use the buyer has for the stocks, and of course different buyers will have different uses.

Consider the statement below:

Fixed assets: premises, plant and equipment	£500,000,000
Depreciation provided	(£300,000,000)
Goodwill	£90,000,000
Current assets: stocks (at lower of cost or net realisable value)	£40,000,000
Current assets: debtors, cash at bank and petty cash	£70,000,000
Current liabilities: amounts owing to suppliers	(£100,000,000)
Total net assets	**£300,000,000**
Deduct goodwill included in the above	£90,000,000
Total tangible assets less current liabilities	**£210,000,000**
Five-year term loan	(£130,000,000)
Net asset value	£80,000,000
Number of ordinary shares	4,000,000
Net asset value per share	£20

In this example the intangible asset of goodwill has been deducted to give a net asset value per share of £20. This is because it has been assumed that the buyer will not have a value for goodwill. Another buyer, however, may indeed have a value for goodwill. If a buyer does value the seller's goodwill, the basis of the goodwill valuation needs to be examined in great detail and it is likely to be contested. For example, if the goodwill relates to the brand being purchased, does it really have value to the buyer, or will the buyer be dropping the brand in favour of its own brand? If the goodwill relates to customers, does this relate entirely to the seller's relationship? Is it transferable or will it be lost upon purchase of the business?

In this example stocks have been valued in accordance with generally accepted accounting principles (GAAP). This may not be their real value to this particular buyer or to the general market of business buyers. A buyer may intend simply to dispose of stocks at a low price. Alternatively, the buyer may have use for the stock at an even higher value than is recorded in the seller's accounts.

You will notice that fixed assets are in the accounts at their net book value of £200 million (£500 million at cost less £300 million of depreciation provided). However, what are these fixed assets really worth? What is their realisable value? What is their value assuming the business is a going concern? What income can they generate, what is their current replacement cost, what is their expected life and what real value do they have to various buyers? Their real value could be a very different from their book value of £200 million.

Generally, an asset-based valuation using financial statements provides a useful floor value and starting point. It certainly lists items for consideration and provides some structure for further analysis for a business valuation. An asset-based valuation can also be used to compare with various earnings-based valuations and raise questions as to whether the assets are being fully utilised. Would the business for sale attract asset strippers?

Valuations based on earnings

Earnings-based or profits-based business valuations enable buyers to estimate possible future returns on a proposed investment. It is assumed that the business is a going concern and will continue to make profits in the future. Asset-based valuations are also used to bring earnings valuations back to a more fundamental and possibly down-to-earth view.

There are two commonly used methods for earnings-based valuations:

Price/earnings ratio

Market value = earnings per share × price/earnings ratio
(or MV = EPS × P/E ratio)

Where:

$$EPS = \frac{\text{Profit attributable to ordinary shareholders}}{\text{Weighted average number of ordinary shares}}$$

$$\text{P/E ratio} = \frac{\text{Market value}}{\text{Earnings per share}}$$

Earnings yield

$$\text{Earnings yield} = \frac{\text{Earnings per share}}{\text{Market price per share as a \%}}$$

$$\text{Market value} = \frac{\text{Earnings}}{\text{Earnings yield}}$$

Valuations based on cash flow

Dividend valuation model

$$\text{Market value (ex div)} = \frac{\text{Annual dividend expected in perpetuity}}{\text{Shareholders' required rate of return}}$$

The basic assumption in this method is that the equilibrium price for a share on the market is the discounted expected future income stream. The expected future income stream for a share is the expected future dividend received in perpetuity. The equilibrium price is the present value of the future income stream.

Dividend growth model

$$\text{Market value} = \frac{\text{Expected dividend in one year's time}}{\text{Shareholders' required growth rate}}$$

For example, a company pays a dividend of £500,000 which is expected to grow by 4% per year. The shareholders require a return of 10% per year. Using the dividend growth model, the value of the business would be:

$$MV = \frac{£500,000 \ (1.04)}{0.10}$$

$$MV = £5,200,000$$

Valuations using discounted cash flow (DCF)

DCF valuation methods simply discount the expected future cash flow from an investment using the cost of capital after tax as a discount rate. For example, an investor expects to receive returns of £50,000 per year in years 0–2 and £40,000 in year 3. It has a cost of capital after tax of 9% during the entire period. Using the DCF method, the value of the investment would be:

Year	Cash flow	Discount factor 9%	Present value £
0	£50,000	1.000	50,000
1	£50,000	0.917	45,850
2	£50,000	0.842	42,100
3	£40,000	0.772	30,880
Net present value			168,830

The DCF method of valuation has indicated that the investor would not want to pay more than £168,830 for this business. However, the value of the same cash flow to other investors might be different because they might use a different cost of capital as a discount factor.

Discounted cash flow methods of business valuation require the use of a discount factor, which in the above example is the business cost of capital. The cost of capital is the return that the business expects to pay to its providers of funds. This will reflect the perceived risk of providing the funds. Business funds will come from a variety of sources and these will have to be considered when determining an average or marginal cost of capital.

7 Compare valuations

It can often be helpful to obtain the financial statements for a company and prepare valuations using these three methods:

- asset-based valuation
- earnings yield
- discounted cash flow.

Consider the results and try to explain the differences between them. Think about how each valuation might relate to different classes of buyer. If you are selling a business, compare the valuations with the lowest price you are prepared to accept and consider whether the need to sell is urgent. If you are buying a business, consider the seller's motives for selling and think about the value of the business.

As a manager you should avoid:

- assuming that there is one simple approach to business valuations
- forgetting that a business has different values for different buyers
- relying on inappropriate and oversimplified online valuation tools
- choosing the wrong valuer
- doing anything that will reduce the value of your business when valuing or seeking a buyer – valuation and sales processes may need to be kept confidential to protect value.

Shareholder value analysis

Shareholder value analysis (SVA) is used to measure shareholder value. This is done by estimating the total net value of a company and dividing it by the value of shares. The result is the shareholder value of the company.

SVA is one of a number of methods used as a substitute for traditional business measurements. It involves calculating a company's value through its returns to shareholders, and is based on the view that the main objective of the directors should be maximising the company's shareholders' wealth. This view has been challenged in recent years, as some argue that the main objective of a company is to serve its customers, and that an overemphasis on maximising shareholder value can lead to less profit and less success for a company, and in extreme cases bankruptcy.

Proponents of SVA suggest that traditional financial methods for calculating business value (such as earnings per share, growth in profits or return on equity) are cost-based, bear little relation to the economic income generated during a period, and are too short term and too focused on past results. SVA is focused on measuring and managing cash flows over time, and provides a longer-term view on which to base strategic decisions.

The principle underlying shareholder value is that companies add value for shareholders only when their equity returns exceed equity costs. Once the amount of value is calculated, improvement targets can be set and shareholder value can be used as a performance measure.

SVA is a universal approach, not subject to particular accounting policies. It is applicable internationally and across sectors. In short, SVA enforces a focus on the future, on customers and especially on the value of future cash flows. However, it can be extremely difficult to calculate future cash flows accurately, and this can lead to incorrect or misleading figures forming the basis for strategic decisions. This checklist introduces the financial calculations involved in carrying out SVA and advises on its implementation.

Action checklist

1 Understand and calculate the organisation's shareholder value

When planning to adopt shareholder value as a financial objective, make sure that you understand the implications and are clear that this is the best approach for your business. Plan your approach first with professional accountants or consultants who specialise in SVA.

A company's shareholder value can be calculated as follows:

Shareholder value = Total business value – Debt

In other words, the value given to shareholders is found by subtracting the market value of debts owed to the company from the total value of the company.

The 'total business value' has three main components:

- present value of future cash flows during a planned period
- residual value of future cash flows from a period beyond the planned period
- weighted average cost of capital.

This is represented in the following equation:

$$\text{Total business value} = \frac{\text{Present value of cash flows} + \text{Residual value of future cash flows}}{\text{Weighted average cost of capital}}$$

If the result of this equation is greater than 1, the company is worth more than the invested capital and value is being created.

Future cash flows

Future cash flows are affected by growth, returns and risk, and these aspects can be explained by seven key value drivers, as described by Alfred Rappaport in his classic book *Creating Shareholder Value: a Guide for Managers and Investors* (revised edition, Free Press, 1998). These drivers must be managed in order to maximise shareholder value:

- sales growth rate
- operating profit margin
- income tax rate
- working capital investment
- fixed capital investment
- cost of capital
- value growth duration.

Residual value

The residual value is an important figure, which represents cash flows arising after the normal planning period. It has been estimated that as much as two-thirds of the value of a business can be attributed to cash flows arising after the normal planning period (usually 5–10 years). Viewed another way, only one-third of the value of a business results from cash flows arising during the normal planning period.

Weighted average cost of capital (WACC)

The WACC is the cost of equity added to the cost of debt, and expresses the return that must be earned to justify the financial resources used. It therefore expresses the opportunity cost of assets in use. It is also entirely market-driven – if the assets cannot earn the required return, investors will withdraw funds from the business.

2 Gain the commitment of senior management

SVA is based on the belief that creation and maximisation of shareholder value is the most important measure of business performance. Senior managers must accept this overriding objective if it is to take root in the organisation and be achieved. There should also be an acceptance that traditional measures and approaches may fall short of achieving this objective.

3 Identify the key value drivers of the organisation and set targets

Unlocking shareholder value is about maximising cash flows. The key value drivers of the business need to be identified. For example, improvements in profit margins could be affected by sales and expenses. These in turn are driven by other factors, such as distribution or selling, which are subject to further influences. This analysis of value drivers links financial and operational objectives and provides a framework for:

- setting targets for performance
- assigning responsibility to individual managers
- reviewing and benchmarking financial performance
- developing strategic plans – the effects on shareholder value of different strategies can be compared by calculating differences between the present value of future cash flows before and after implementation.

Identification of key factors influencing value drivers is often a process of trial and error, but it must be undertaken in order to improve cash flows.

4 Communicate the approach and train staff

The technical aspects of SVA are unlikely to concern managers, but they need to understand the broad nature of shareholder value creation (especially for project appraisal) and be able to identify value drivers and improve their performance.

Adopting SVA and setting new targets are likely to challenge existing managerial habits and approaches. Resistance may result, and previous approaches will need to be re-evaluated and possibly discarded for new targets.

Unlocking shareholder value is essentially a change process, and line managers usually make the key operational decisions. Training will increase their likelihood of achieving early successes that show the value of the new approach.

5 Change information systems to monitor and measure progress

Information systems (especially financial reporting systems) may need revising for SVA, as conventional reporting systems may not give the information or the formats required. To unlock shareholder value, information systems must provide data to measure and monitor key value drivers and targets.

6 Change the financial incentive schemes used for managers

Align incentive schemes with SVA to encourage senior managers to increase shareholder value over realistic time periods, and not focus only on short-term profit, growth or earnings per share. Line managers' incentives and bonuses should encourage control over value drivers.

7 Monitor and review progress and refine targets

Creation of sustained value requires constant monitoring. Appraisals, performance reviews, management meetings and key decisions should focus on progress achieved and actions required to continue increasing shareholder value. Failure to emphasise value creation can result in managers focusing on targets that have become irrelevant, or that now undermine the long-term value of the business.

As a manager you should avoid:

- limited resourcing – developing and implementing SVA can be complex

- impatience – time, energy and commitment are needed (some estimates claim two years is the norm)

- being half-hearted or hesitant – make sure that you know what improvements you want and what needs to be done to achieve them.

Management accounting

Management accounting is a practice that provides the managers of a business with the information they need to make decisions. It encompasses performance management, strategic management and risk management.

Management accounting is concerned with using financial information to assist in the internal management of an organisation. It is different from financial accounting, which provides financial reports for various segments of the public and for shareholders. This checklist is intended to give managers an overview of the scope of the work done by management accountants and the contribution it can make to the effective management and performance improvement of a business.

Action checklist

1 Understand the scope of management accounting

Management accounting seeks to address these three business areas:

- performance management
- strategic management
- risk management.

There is of course, considerable overlap between them. Although management accounting as a discipline and practice is distinct from financial accounting, it may use information produced in a business's financial accounts and a certain level of integration is required.

2 Understand the role of management accounting in performance management

Management accounting seeks to assist the management of performance through a process of reporting on all aspects of business activity. This includes reporting on:

- sales – volumes sold, product mixes and prices
- manufacturing efficiency – material usage, material prices, labour efficiency, labour rates and capacity usage
- administration – overhead expenditure, departmental budgets and cash management.

The precise scope of a management accountant's work varies from one organisation to another. In smaller organisations the financial accountant may also be responsible for the production of management reports.

Two significant areas of a management accountant's responsibility are product costing and budgetary control.

Costing

The elements of a product cost are direct material, direct labour, direct and apportioned overheads. Some costs are variable in that they 'vary' with a level of activity, such as production volumes; other costs are fixed and do not vary with activity, such as rates.

A management accountant might prepare product costs on a marginal costing basis and only allocate variable costs (direct material and direct labour) to the product.

On the following page is an example of marginal costing.

	Product A	Product B	Total
Unit selling price	£300	£500	
Unit variable cost (material/labour)	£100	£200	
Unit contribution	£200	£300	
Gross margin	67%	60%	
Sales volume	100	50	
Total contribution	£20,000	£15,000	£35,000
Fixed costs: overheads			£20,000
Net profit			£15,000

Marginal costing clearly demonstrates the break-even point (BEP). In this case the business needs to make a contribution of £20,000 to fully cover the fixed costs and break even.

Alternatively, a management accountant might prepare costs on a fully absorbed basis and allocate the £20,000 of fixed costs to the products.

One method of absorption costing is the fully integrated standard costing system that is used in manufacturing companies. This method uses standard costs, material usage, labour rates and times for product costing and produces reports that show variances for each of these categories, enabling managers to take corrective action or amend plans.

Another method is activity-based costing (ABC), whereby costs are first assigned to activities and then to products.

Budgeting

Budgetary control falls within the performance management and control aspects of management accounting. A budget is a financial evaluation of a plan against which actual expenditure can be compared and monitored. A typical budget report will show actual costs against budgeted costs and provide an explanation for any variance.

Variance analysis is a technique used in management accounting to analyse variances against budget.

For example:

Budget v. actual – Finance dept. – Year to 30 Sept. 2013 – £'000

Category	Budget	Actual	Variance	A/O	Rate	Timing
Salaries	10	12	(2)	(1)	(1)	0
Travel	2	0	2	0	0	2
Total	12	12	0	(1)	(1)	2

A/O = additional outlay (extra staff member)
Rate = higher rate paid to budgeted staff
Timing = expenditure slipped
Note: Although the current total variance is 0, it will be (2) adverse once the planned travel is undertaken. This variance is due to an additional staff member (additional outlay) and a pay increase above that budgeted (rate).

Performance indicators

In addition to costing and budgeting, performance management is concerned with all aspects of a business's activities. A management accountant will produce reports on any area that is relevant to the business. Key performance measures will be identified and reported on a management dashboard.

Some key performance figures include:

- sales value
- sales volume/mix
- gross margins
- market share
- manufacturing costs
- material price and usage
- labour rates and efficiency
- capacity usage
- stock turnover
- expenditure variance analysis
- cash levels and liquidity

- debtor days
- gearing ratio (loans to equity)
- net profit
- return on capital employed in the business
- dividend yield and cover.

Business managers should identify the most important performance indicators that are needed on a daily basis, and make sure that the management reporting system is capable of providing the information required. Three of the most common daily internal indicators are cash, sales and gross margin. These, along with external information such as share price, are always closely monitored by the chief executive. It is important to identify, collect and take relevant information into account when making business decisions.

3 Understand the role of management accounting in strategic management

Management accounting provides information to guide the strategic direction of a business. This includes helping a business decide on which potential investments to pursue and setting selling prices, marketing strategy, funding, dividend policy and financial strategy. The most important interfaces between management accounting and strategic management are discussed below.

Setting selling prices

Selling prices are determined by external market forces. However, internal management accounting information enables decisions to be made concerning which products to sell and how profitable they will be. It also helps with product sales/mix decisions. The process for setting selling prices involves a comparison of market prices obtainable with internal costs of sales. This enables decisions to be made regarding the full range of internal processes from buying to manufacturing and distribution.

Pricing strategies are a part of business strategy and management accounting information will help identify the benefits of each strategy.

Investment appraisal

Management accounting can provide a process for analysing and making various investment decisions. The most important thing to remember in any investment decision is relevant cash flow. It is important not to get confused by information and values that are simply not relevant.

Management accounting uses a number of techniques to evaluate and prioritise potential investments. These include payback period, return on capital, accounting rate of return, discounted cash flow, the internal rate of return and capital rationing techniques.

Make-or-buy and lease-or-buy decisions:

Whether to make a product internally or buy it externally is a common decision that organisations have to make. Another is whether to lease or buy. These options will invariably have different cash flow timings and taxation considerations. Then there are questions of capacity and opportunity costs. Management accounting can extract and obtain the relevant information and prepare the calculations (using discounted cash flow and other techniques) to enable a correct decision to be made.

Gearing and the cost of capital

How an organisation is to be financed is a key strategic decision. Should it be highly geared or low geared? This decision requires an understanding of the cost of capital – the return that an organisation has to pay to gain and retain funds from investors. Investors assess risk. The management accountant should be able to calculate the weighted average cost of capital (WACC), the marginal cost of capital and the cost of ordinary share capital, and use the dividend growth model and capital-asset pricing model (CAPM). A detailed explanation of these concepts is not possible within this short checklist, but managers should understand how they are used in strategic financial decision-making and in providing discount rates within discounted cash flow calculations.

Dividend policy

This can have a huge impact on the financial health of a company. It affects liquidity, the cost of capital and the market value of shares. Retained earnings are a most important source of finance. A balance needs to be struck between shareholder and market expectations and financial efficiency. Management accounting will help businesses to arrive at an optimal solution for dividend payments.

4 Understand the role of management accounting in risk management

Management accountants are trained in analysis and control and have an important role to play in the identification and management of risk. They can assist managers in prioritising business risks, evaluating them and determining the extent to which they can be controlled or mitigated.

Risk is inherent in all business activities and, generally, the greater the risk the greater the potential return or loss. Some risks are not at all obvious and can catch a business by surprise. Management accounting provides a series of tools and techniques that help identify and evaluate risks.

A risk-based approach to managing an enterprise (such as enterprise risk management, or ERM) attempts to provide an explanation of risk to various stakeholders in an organisation by identifying events that might occur in the pursuit of organisational objectives and assessing their probability and financial or other impacts.

Some risks may be likely to occur but may have only a low impact on business performance or results. Other risks may be less likely but may have a much greater impact on the business. Some risks may be highly probable and also have a high impact on results. Risks can be plotted against their probability to determine where most management attention should be focused so as to avoid or limit damage.

Once risks have been prioritised control can be exercised. However, some risks are less easy to control than others. Some risks may be neither controllable nor avoidable. Management accounting provides a framework for the classification and better understanding of risk.

As a manager you should avoid:

- solving the wrong problem really well
- getting 'bogged down' with irrelevant information
- complex spreadsheets with embedded errors.

Increasing profitability

In its simplest form, a profit is the excess of total revenue over total costs during a specific period. It is the task of managers to seek to improve profitability and to achieve a level of profit commensurate with the level of risk involved. For any business the objective of making a surplus of revenues in excess of costs is a commercial imperative.

Although many factors can contribute to the profitability of a business, this checklist focuses on five important ones. Most managers will be familiar with these strategic routes, which are frequently taken in pursuit of greater profitability, but they may fail to recognise the interrelationships between them.

The five basic ways in which an organisation can have a direct effect on its profitability are:

- increasing sales volume
- reducing costs and/or ensuring that costs are fully recovered
- improving the product mix
- raising prices
- reducing the capital employed in the business.

A change in any one of these will have an impact on the others. Any change made or planned, whether voluntary or involuntary, must therefore be considered in the context of all the others; changes made in isolation may not have the expected impact on profitability.

There are distinct advantages in recognising the main interrelationships between the five strategic factors, and working with these, so that:

- financial planning will take all five factors and their interrelationships into account
- the impact on profitability of changes can be assessed systematically
- the risks associated with changes can be viewed more realistically
- the line between risk taking and recklessness can become clearer.

Action checklist

1 Carry out a market analysis

Take a close look at current and potential markets, using focus groups, customer feedback and commercial and commissioned market research. Bear in mind that in certain product and service areas, technological innovations can change or have a significant impact on market structures and loyalty quickly. Market analysis, therefore, has to be targeted to give rapid results. This research should reveal whether your current markets are good enough and identify new markets to penetrate.

2 Consider increasing your sales volume

Increasing sales volume may appear to be an easy way of increasing the profitability of your organisation, but this is not necessarily the case. There are certain points that must be recognised:

- Selling more and more is not the key to increased profitability. Profit requires turnover, but turnover does not equal profit.

Alternative US and IAS accounting terms are also in use – see page xi for a short list.

- If you increase your sales volume, you must simultaneously control costs, prices, capital employed and your product/service mix. Make sure that none of the latter components of your potential profitability increase disproportionately; if they do, increased sales will lead to a reduction rather than an increase in profit.

- Seeking to increase your sales turnover by employing an additional representative or trading in a bigger geographical area will only produce more profit if extra sales produce at least enough extra profit (not turnover) to cover the extra costs.

- If prices and margins are reduced to generate more sales, a considerable increase in sales will be necessary; otherwise total turnover will fall while costs remain the same.

- Increases in small volume orders may hinder profitability rather than boost it due to the inherent order administration costs, such as invoicing and dispatching.

- If credit is extended to encourage more sales, your organisation will have to bear the costs of this – with a knock-on effect on profitability.

- Selling more of all your product/service lines and/or introducing new ones may increase your sales volume, but make sure you know the contribution that each product/service line makes. Selling more of loss-making lines is bad business unless it is necessary to raise sales of profit-making ones.

- In some circumstances greater profits may be achieved if turnover is reduced. Surveys have shown that a wholly disproportionate amount of cost and effort can be invested to achieve a small amount of turnover and sales revenue – it is not uncommon to find that 50% of deliveries account for only 15% of sales revenue. Consider what would happen if you reduced your sales by a selective 10%.

3 Look at the possibility of reducing your costs

Investigate and establish your true costs in total and for unit sales. You cannot adjust your costs in relation to other parts of your business unless you know what they are. Consider the effects of specific cost reductions carefully – arbitrary reductions may not produce the desired results in the long term. Seek advice from your accountant, your auditors and your bank.

Where appropriate, compare the lead time of products compared with the operation time required to make them; the gap reveals the opportunity to improve your performance. Focus in particular on evaluating and eliminating waste within your organisation. There are traditionally seven categories of waste: overproduction, waiting, transporting, inappropriate processing, unnecessary inventory, unnecessary motions and defects. An eighth would be underusing your employees' talent.

4 Analyse and improve your product or service mix

Product or service mix is the combination in which the products or services you provide are sold. The mix is normally derived from a series of historical accidents rather than from careful planning and analysis, and consequently may not be the most profitable for your organisation.

Examine the products sold by your organisation in terms of the costs attributable to each and the net margin each makes. You may find that the products that produce the highest unit gross profit and make the highest percentage contribution to your volume of sales also attract a disproportionate amount of your selling costs.

You may find, for example, that you should aim to sell more of A and B, which you have found to be profitable, to supply less of C and D, which are of limited profitability, and to eliminate E and F from your sales portfolio as they are loss-makers. Consider the impact this will have on other factors – for example, a well-founded change in the product/service mix may lead to a reduced volume of sales but increased profitability.

5 Examine your selling prices and profit margins

Raising selling prices is a potential route to increased profitability (or to maintaining current levels of profitability when they might otherwise fall), but there are pitfalls. Price increases may be accepted if they are part of a general adjustment of prices in your business sector, in which case your overall level of profitability is likely to be merely maintained. To raise prices in isolation without losing business requires a near monopoly situation, a clear difference between your products and those of your competitors, or a carefully thought-out policy and sales strategy.

6 Look at the capital employed in your business

Obtaining good returns on capital and reducing the capital tied up in your business normally leads to improved profitability. Identify the categories of capital employed in your business and consider whether the following actions could be applied to these categories:

- introducing tighter control of credit
- reducing stock levels
- introducing outsourcing or expanding its scope
- disposing of redundant buildings or even relocating to a new site, where better lease terms may be available
- maximising the benefits of exploiting information and communications technologies
- making sure you take professional advice.

7 Remember balance

A healthy business in a competitive environment is always changing, and as demonstrated here, this is particularly relevant to the five components of profitability and their interrelationships. Change, particularly in the area of aiming to improve profitability, always requires compromise, and you must aim to achieve the best balance possible between sales volume, costs, margins, product mix and capital employed.

As a manager you should avoid:

- ignoring the 'bad news' which may emerge from analysis, especially when this threatens the achievement of a pet ambition, such as expansion into other lines or another country

- ignoring changes which may be imposed on your business, for example by your bank or through legislation.

Investment appraisal

Investment appraisal is an exercise involving a wide-ranging analysis of all the factors to be taken into account when considering an investment in a capital project to assess whether it is worthwhile to make an investment.

In today's competitive business environment, getting the most from the resources available is one of the keys to business success. Making decisions about investment is one of the most important long-term issues for any business and represents a major challenge for management, particularly in times of change and uncertainty.

Investment has traditionally been divided into capital expenditure (property, plant, equipment, etc) and revenue expenditure (materials, wages, selling costs, etc). In the knowledge age, expenditure related to the training and development of employees should also be seen as a strategic investment for the future.

Investment is the purchase or creation of assets with the objective of making gains in the future. The benefits of investment may be financial, tangible non-financial (such as staff retention), or intangible (staff morale, public reputation, etc). This checklist outlines a traditional approach to assessing investment opportunities focusing on the benefits in purely financial terms.

Paul King (who has been described as having devised one of the best methods for making capital investment decisions) defined a capital budgeting process in his 1975 paper 'Strategic Control of Capital Expenditure'. He identified six stages for capital investment decisions and concluded that decisions emerged as a result of a complex social process of which formal consideration by management formed only a part. The six stages are:

- triggering – recognition of opportunities
- screening – initial screening as to whether or not to pursue further
- definition – identification of alternatives, strategic fit
- evaluation – analysis, DCF, NPV, payback, IRR, ARR (all explained below)
- transmission – communicating and gaining commitment across the wider organisation
- decision – evaluation of choices and choosing between them.

Key considerations in making investment decisions include:

- What is the scale of the investment and can the company afford it?
- How long will it be before the investment starts to yield returns?
- How long will it take to pay back the investment?
- What are the expected profits from the investment?
- Could the money that is being ploughed into the investment yield higher returns elsewhere?

Carrying out an investment appraisal helps to ensure that cash and other resources are invested in the most profitable projects, realistic project budgets are established, and risks arising from the investment are considered, so that measures can be taken to eliminate or mitigate them. Failure to conduct investment appraisals (or the conduct of inadequate appraisals) could mean that cash and other resources are invested in suboptimal projects and subjective and unfair decisions may be made. However, it is worth bearing in mind that the financial benefits of investment are often overestimated and may turn out to be lower than anticipated, even when using the techniques outlined here. A number of alternative approaches have been proposed but have not yet been widely adopted.

A mix of skills is required when conducting investment appraisals, including the ability to gather information, carry out financial analysis, write a business plan and make recommendations – all of which are key management skills.

Action checklist

1 Identify the key plans and objectives for the organisation

Identify objectives and plans so that you can assess whether your investment proposal fits in with them:

- consider whether there are alternatives to your proposal
- assess the duration of the project and list all estimated payments and receipts relevant to it.

Some payments and receipts are relatively straightforward to identify. For instance, an investment in a new retail store will lead to cash receipts from sales over a number of years and payments for staff wages, maintenance, goods for resale, and so on. As tax payments or tax receipts and inflation should also be considered, you may need the help of an accountant.

Other costs and benefits arising from the investment are more difficult to identify and estimate. For example, an investment in a high-tech system may lead to an increase in productivity and morale. If costs and benefits such as these are difficult to quantify in monetary terms, notes should be attached to the investment appraisal to highlight them.

2 Produce a cash flow forecast and profit and loss account for the project

A cash flow forecast that allocates receipts and payments to months (or years) should be produced. If you intend to calculate the accounting rate of return, a forecast profit and loss account also needs to be produced. This also needs to be segregated into months (or years).

3 Understand the methods used to appraise investments

The most common methods of investment appraisal are listed below. They can be divided into those that use cash flow forecasts and those that use profit and loss account forecasts.

Methods that use cash flow forecasts

Payback point. This measures the point at which cumulative cash receipts equal cumulative payments. Proposals with a shorter payback period are generally preferred.

For example, a company is considering purchasing an asset. At the outset it will pay out £100,000 and have inflows of £70,000 after a year and a further £52,000 after two years. At this point, the asset will be scrapped. The company applies a discount rate of 10% when calculating net present value.

Should the company make the investment?

The payback point is when cumulative outflows equal cumulative inflows – that is, the point at which the project starts to make a surplus. In the example below, all figures are £'000.

	Outset	Year 1	Year 2	Total
Inflows	–	70.0	52.0	122.0
Outflows	(100.0)	–	–	(100.0)
Net	(100.0)	70.0	52.0	22.0
Cumulative cash flow	(100.0)	(30.0)	22.0	

The payback point appears sometime during year 2. Assuming that the inflow of £52,000 occurs evenly during year 2, the company can estimate the point at which payback occurs. It needs £30,000 of the £52,000 to reach that point. This occurs after 30/52ths of year 2, or after 30 weeks, or after 30/52 × 12 = 7 months of year 2. The payback period is therefore 1 year and 7 months.

Net present value (NPV). This method recognises that:

- the organisation has a cost of capital – that is, the cash for the investment is borrowed and therefore interest needs to be paid on the borrowing
- cash receipts and payments in the future may be subject to inflation
- some investments may be riskier than others – for instance, it is riskier for a company to diversify into a new product or service.

After considering these points, a discount rate will be decided upon and applied to the cash flow forecast to give the net present value of the project – that is, the return from the project in today's values. Proposals with a higher net present value are generally preferred.

In the example below, all figures are £'000 except the discount factor, which is taken from published discount tables.

	Now	**Year 1**	**Year 2**	**Total**
Inflows	–	70.0	52.0	122.0
Outflows	(100.0)	–	–	(100.0)
Net (a)	(100.0)	70.0	52.0	22.0
Discount factor @ 10% (b)	1.000	0.909	0.826	
NPV (a × b)	(100.0)	63.6	42.9	6.5

The project has a net present value of £6,500. This means that after allowing for the cost of borrowing at 10%, the project still makes a surplus of £6,500 at today's value.

Internal rate of return (IRR). This method uses discounting techniques (see net present value above) to calculate the percentage return from an investment. Proposals with a higher IRR are generally preferred.

We know from the net present value calculation that the project will make sufficient returns to pay interest on borrowings at 10% and still make a surplus. The internal rate of return of the project is the borrowing rate that the project could just afford to pay, or, perhaps, the actual rate of return on the project. Looking at this in another way, it is the discount factor that is used to produce a project NPV of zero.

It is possible to arrive at an IRR by trial and error – by changing the discount factor until it produces an NPV of nil. In this case, the IRR is 15%.

In the example below, all figures are £'000 except the discount factor, which is taken from published discount tables.

	Now	Year 1	Year 2	Total
Inflows	–	70.0	52.0	122.0
Outflows	(100.0)	–	–	(100.0)
Net (a)	(100.0)	70.0	52.0	22.0
Discount factor @ 15% (b)	1.000	0.869	0.756	
NPV (a × b)	100.0	60.8	39.3	0.1

Note that the total is approximately nil.

Method that uses profit and loss account forecasts

Accounting rate of return (ARR). This calculates a percentage return that is similar to return on capital employed. Proposals with a higher ARR are generally preferred. You may need to ask an accountant to assist with these methods. Spreadsheets can usually calculate the NPV and IRR for you.

In the project profit and loss account example below, all figures are £'000.

	Year 1	Year 2	Total
Sales	70	52	122
Costs			
Depreciation	50	50	100
Profit	20	2	22

The accounting rate of return calculation is shown below.

$$\frac{\text{Average return (profit)}}{\text{Average invested}} = \frac{(\pounds20,000 + \pounds2,000) \div 2}{\pounds100,000 \div 2} \times 100$$

$$\frac{\pounds11,000}{\pounds50,000} \times 100(\%) = 22\%$$

This shows the average amount invested over the lifetime of the asset. If the amount invested at the start is assumed to be £100,000, and the amount invested is assumed to be nil at the end of the project, the average amount invested will be £50,000.

Why would companies wish to consider the accounting rate of return rather than the simpler methods of payback, net present value and internal rate of return?

Internal and external analysts usually use profit and loss accounts to measure the performance of the business. They will calculate ratios such as return on capital employed (ROCE). The ARR gives an approximation for an asset purchase or project and the effect on the company's overall ROCE can be assessed. If the asset purchase (or project) rate of return is higher than the company's normal ROCE, it is likely to be accepted.

4 Decide whether you should make the investment

Among other things, you should consider whether the company has (or can obtain) the initial cash to purchase the asset. You should also consider other possible investments using some or all of the above techniques. You will probably invest in assets (or projects) that have a:

- shorter payback period
- higher net present value
- higher internal rate of return
- higher accounting rate of return.

5 Include your calculations in a business plan for your proposal

Any substantial investment proposal should be incorporated into either the department's overall business plan or a separate plan, which, in addition to the purely financial calculations, should detail the costs (staff, time) and anticipated non-financial benefits, such as greater efficiency.

As a manager you should avoid:

- forgetting to consider inflation, taxation and risks
- forgetting to consider alternatives to your proposal
- not giving full consideration to non-financial factors, such as increase in morale
- failing to enlist the help of an accountant.

Discounted cash flow

Discounted cash flow (DCF) is a method of capital investment appraisal used for comparing alternative investment opportunities. Central to discounted cash flow is the assumption that money paid out today is of more value than money paid out in the future, and that the longer it is before the money is paid out the less valuable it is. This should be readily apparent. For example, banks pay interest on money deposited with them and charge interest on money borrowed from them.

Cash receipts and payments expected in the future are discounted to bring them back to 'present value'. The longer the wait before money is received or a payment is made, the bigger the discounting factor that is used.

As a technique for the appraisal of capital investments, such as major projects or programmes, DCF is of critical importance when the capital to be invested is significant or the term of the investment is more than two or three years. DCF is widely regarded as superior to other capital investment appraisal methods such as payback and return on investment because it takes into account the timing of cash flows and helps financial managers make decisions based on real returns from investment. This is particularly important for investments and returns that span many years, and where the cost of money is high.

This checklist describes, with examples, the principles for calculating the DCF for any capital investment for a number of years ahead.

Action checklist

1 Extracts from interest rate tables

Interest rate tables are widely available. The following extracts indicate the principles and will be used in the examples in this checklist.

Interest rate

Year	10%	12%	14%	16%
1	0.91	0.89	0.88	0.86
2	0.83	0.80	0.77	0.74
3	0.75	0.71	0.67	0.64
4	0.68	0.64	0.59	0.55

The interest rates have been rounded and so the figures used in the examples will also be rounded. A greater degree of accuracy can be obtained by using tables that go to a higher number of decimal places.

2 Present value explained

A simple example will show how, if an interest rate of 10% is used, £1,000 becomes £1,210 in two years and £1,331 in three years.

	£
Present value	1,000
Year 1 (10% × £1,000)	100
	1,100
Year 2 (10% × £1,100)	110
	1,210
Year 3 (10% × £1,210)	121
	1,331

A glance at the interest tables shows that a factor of 0.75 must be used, assuming an interest rate of 10%, to bring £1,331 received in three years' time to present value. After allowing for rounding, £1,331 × 0.75 = £1,000.

There is a convenient formula that may be used as an alternative to interest rate tables:

$$\text{Present value} = \frac{\text{Future sum}}{(1 + r)^n}$$

where r is the rate of interest expressed as a decimal (0.10 for 10%), and n is the number of years.

This can be proved by using the formula as a substitute for the above three-stage calculation:

$$£1,000 = \frac{1,331}{(1 + 0.1)^3}$$

The formula may be particularly useful if you wish to do a complicated calculation involving a lengthy period. Suppose, for example, you want to know, assuming an interest rate of 13.4%, the present value of £16,784 to be received in 14 years' time. The calculation is:

$$£2,886 = \frac{16,784}{(1 + 0.134)^{14}}$$

This is a compelling example of the effect of compound interest. It could also serve as a thought-provoking illustration of how it may be necessary to build up a large capital sum at a future date to fund a comfortable retirement as measured in today's money.

3 A practical example of an investment decision

The principles can best be illustrated with a practical example. A manufacturer must replace a machine immediately, and three options are being considered:

● Machine A will cost £100,000 and is expected to have a trade-in value after four years of £15,000. It will achieve operating savings of £35,000 in each of the four years.

● Machine B will cost £80,000 and is expected to have a trade-in value after four years of £30,000. It will achieve operating savings of £29,000 in each of the four years.

● Machine C will cost £140,000 and is expected to have a trade-in value after four years of £82,000. It will achieve operating savings of £38,000 in each of the four years.

Note that over the four-year period the undiscounted cash flow consequences are:

- Machine A – £55,000 favourable
- Machine B – £66,000 favourable
- Machine C – £94,000 favourable.

On this basis machine C is the best buy, but what happens if the cash receipts are discounted? Assume that a discount factor of 16% is appropriate and, rather unrealistically, but to keep the calculations as simple as possible, that all the savings are made at the end of each year. The calculations are as follows:

	Machine A	Machine B	Machine C
	£	£	£
Expenditure now	100,000	80,000	140,000
Less year 1 savings (discounted)	30,100	24,940	2,680
	69,900	55,060	107,320
Less year 2 savings (discounted)	25,900	21,460	28,120
	44,000	33,600	79,200
Less year 3 savings (discounted)	22,400	18,560	24,320
	21,600	15,040	54,880
Less year 4 savings (discounted)	19,250	15,950	20,900
	2,350	(910)	33,980
Less trade-in value (discounted)	8,250	16,500	45,100
	(5,900)	(17,410)	(11,120)

It will be seen that after discounting at 16% a different result is obtained. On this basis machine B is the best, but before leaving the example it is worth reworking the figures using a different discount factor. The following calculations are based on 12%:

	Machine A	Machine B	Machine C
	£	£	£
Expenditure now	100,000	80,000	140,000
Less year 1 savings (discounted)	31,150	25,810	33,820
	68,850	54,190	106,180
Less year 2 savings (discounted)	28,000	23,200	30,400
	40,850	30,990	75,780
Less year 3 savings (discounted)	24,850	20,590	26,980
	16,000	10,400	48,800
Less year 4 savings (discounted)	22,400	18,560	24,320
	(6,400)	(8,160)	24,480
Less trade-in value (discounted)	(9,600)	19,200	52,480
	(16,000)	(27,360)	(28,000)

This gives a different result again. It is practically a dead heat between machine B and machine C, with machine C having only a small advantage. The different results powerfully illustrate the importance of the discount rate selected. The main reason for the difference is that a higher proportion of machine C's cash inflow comes at the end of the period. The lower discount rate results in this having more weight.

4 An important consideration not revealed by discounted cash flow

DCF does not take account of the amount of capital tied up. For example, if a 12% discount factor is used, machine C appears marginally to be the best choice. However, an extra £60,000 is tied up compared with machine B, and unless it has a clear advantage it may well be rejected for this reason.

5 The choice of discount factor to be used

The example illustrates that this can make a significant difference, but unfortunately there are no absolute rules, and each situation should be assessed on its merits. A good starting point is the cost of capital or borrowing. If a company is paying 10% interest on its overdraft, this is the starting point; but of course it is not usually possible to be certain what the cost of borrowing will be in future years. Many people like to feed in a factor that reflects the scarcity of capital and borrowing. For example, an overdraft rate of 10% is of only marginal relevance if the bank is unwilling to lend. Perhaps an extremely sound proposal is being evaluated, but it is competing with other extremely sound proposals for a limited supply of funds. Some managers like to use a high factor to make each project compete and clearly justify itself.

In practice, the discount factor is often chosen through a mixture of scientific calculation and subjective judgement. It is an important and complex subject, which is beyond the remit of this checklist.

6 Using Excel for discounted cash flow

Proficient Excel users will be aware that there is a function for the calculation of discounted cash flow and net present value. Use '*fx*' to find the NPV function under the financial category. This function returns the NPV of an investment based on a discount rate and a series of future payments and income.

Cost benefit analysis

Cost benefit analysis (CBA) is a process for calculating the costs and benefits of a project, decision or policy.

CBA can be used to help managers make sound investment decisions and compare investment options. Discounted cash flow and net present value techniques are used in CBA to make allowance for the time value of money. This checklist explains the process of CBA with an example.

Action checklist

1 Identify potential investment opportunities

Start by drawing up a list of all the relevant projects or investment opportunities and the information relating to them.

2 Determine the value of costs and benefits and time schedule

It is important to consider which costs and income streams are relevant to your decision. In this example, a business has identified an investment opportunity for £300,000 that would yield the following income stream:

Year 1	£110,000
Year 2	£115,000
Year 3	£115,000
Total	**£340,000**

The business has a cost of capital of 4% per year and committed rental costs are £6,000 per year.

3 Decide on an appropriate discount rate

The rate to use is a subject of much debate. It is usually the company's cost of capital. The sum of the present values is calculated using the 4% discount factors provided in the discount table below. In this case the discount rate represents the company's cost of capital.

Discount rates

Years	1%	2%	3%	4%	5%	6%
1	0.990	0.980	0.971	0.962	0.952	0.943
2	0.980	0.961	0.943	0.925	0.907	0.890
3	0.971	0.942	0.915	0.889	0.864	0.840
4	0.961	0.924	0.888	0.855	0.823	0.792

4 Calculate the discounted cash flow and net present value of each alternative

Present value analysis

	Cash flow	Discount factor 4%	Present value
Year 0	−£300,000	1.000	−£300,000
Year 1	£110,000	0.962	£105,820
Year 2	£115,000	0.925	£106,375
Year 3	£115,000	0.889	£102,235
NPV			£14,430

The present value for each year was obtained by multiplying the cash flow value by the discount factor (obtained from the discount table). The present value column was then totalled to give the net present value (NPV). This is a positive figure (£14,430).

Note that costs already committed are not relevant to this decision.

To calculate present values manually the following formula can be used, where PV = present value, and FV = future value:

$$PV = FV \times \frac{1}{(1+r)^n}$$

where r is the discount rate and n is the number of years.

The present value of £115,000 in three years using 4% discount rate is:

$$PV = £115{,}000 \times \frac{1}{(1+0.04)^3}$$

$$PV = £115{,}000 \times \frac{1}{1.125}$$

$$PV = £115{,}000 \times 0.889$$

$$PV = £102{,}235 \text{ (as in the above example)}$$

It is normal practice to use Excel for discounted cash flow analysis and sensitivity analysis. If you are proficient, this will save time and make it easier to carry out the analysis. However, you should understand the mechanics of discounted cash flow and net present value before using programs to do the sums. Know what answer to expect.

5 Undertake a sensitivity analysis on each variable factor

This analysis has assumed certain income streams and costs and a discount rate. There could be other embedded variables and assumptions. To refine the analysis further, it would be prudent to carry out a sensitivity analysis. This will enable you to see how sensitive your answer is to different discount rates and other variable values. In a sensitivity analysis, each variable is replaced with another value and the calculation is then redone to show the effect of this on the final NPV. This is carried out for each variable – one at a time. From this analysis it is possible to answer 'what if?' questions such as: What would happen if the cost of capital increased to 5%? Would this result in a different decision?

6 Make a decision

In the example above, the yield provided is greater than the company's cost of capital. On the basis of NPV analysis the project should be undertaken. However, this assumes that there are no other better projects. If there are other projects, a similar analysis should be undertaken for each project and the project(s) with the best yield should be chosen. It might be necessary to rank projects in order of return if the amount of capital available to invest is limited. Capital rationing will need to be applied.

If the net value in this example had been a negative figure, the project would not have yielded a return greater than the cost of capital and would not be undertaken.

However, it is also important to check what the relevant stakeholders hope to gain from the investment – return on investment might not be the only consideration.

7 Consider the use of alternative methods

There are many other methods that can be used in cost benefit analysis. Each has its merits and weaknesses. Discounted cash flow and net present value are the most widely used and they are academically supported. Other methods that you might wish to explore include the payback period, the return on capital employed, the accounting rate of return and the internal rate of return.

As a manager you should avoid:

- incorrect use of spreadsheets – test your answers manually to avoid embedded errors
- unnecessary complexity in the process
- spending hours arguing over the merits of minor adjustments to discount rates or other variables when the end result might not be sensitive to these factors.

Understanding pricing strategies

Price setting is a series of policy or strategic procedures undertaken by companies to determine and set the price customers should pay to acquire a product or service. Pricing policies and strategies identify and define the factors affecting a company's pricing decisions, including market share, competition, costs, product identity, perceived value of a product to customers and the company's desire to make a profitable return.

Pricing decisions are critical to competitive success as they determine the volume of business a company will achieve, its position in the market compared with competitors, and its total sales, revenues and profit. Pricing is a business activity that can cause disagreement and dissent. It is a difficult task for any business, and incorrectly pricing a product or service can erode or destroy profitability.

For most businesses, pricing decisions involve determining an effective policy for pricing and deciding whether prices should be lower, the same as, or higher than those of their competitors. For most customers, the price is assessed according to the value delivered to them or their business.

Setting a selling price is fundamentally about determining the best price that can be obtained in a market and knowing the lowest price that is acceptable to your business.

This checklist discusses various strategies and approaches to pricing and highlights the main activities in pricing policies and strategies.

Action checklist

1 Pricing strategy

Strategic pricing is the effective, proactive use of product pricing to drive sales and profits. A pricing strategy will enable you to determine how much money can be spent on development, support, promotion and other costs associated with the product or service. There are four basic components to a successful pricing strategy:

- **Costs.** Focus on current and future costs as opposed to past costs to determine the cost basis for your pricing strategy. You should understand the different types of costs, such as fixed and variable costs, which are discussed in further detail in this checklist.

- **Price sensitivity.** Various factors cause the price sensitivities of buyers to shift, and your pricing strategy must shift with them.

- **Competition.** Pay attention to but do not simply copy your competitors.

- **Product life cycle.** How you price, and what you provide for that price, will change as you move through the product life cycle.

Consider testing your prices against those of similar products in the marketplace. It may be wise to test at a higher price first – customers respond well to price reductions, but they will not be so keen if the price is pitched low at first and raised later.

2 Pricing policy

Prices are generally determined by the market forces of supply and demand, not just by cost. However, an understanding of cost is essential in understanding the consequences of price decisions.

A company should have a pricing policy to guide those responsible for pricing decisions (either explicitly recorded or implicitly understood). This policy should include the general principles a company proposes to follow in its pricing activities.

There are three things that managers must understand and take into account in determining a pricing policy:

- **Costs.** To make a profit, a business should make sure that its products are priced above their total average cost. In the short term, it may be acceptable to price below total cost if this price exceeds the marginal cost of production, so that the sale still produces a positive contribution to fixed costs.

- **Competitors.** If the business is a monopolist, it can set any price. At the other extreme, if a business operates under conditions of perfect competition, it has no choice other than to accept the market price. The reality is usually somewhere in between. In such cases the chosen price needs to be carefully considered relative to those of close competitors.

- **Customers.** Customer expectations about price must be addressed. Ideally, a business should attempt to quantify its demand curve to estimate what volume of sales will be achieved at given prices.

Ethical considerations are also important when deciding on a pricing policy. This can have an impact on customer perceptions and contribute to industry profitability and business sustainability.

3 Establish your value factors

Make sure that you take into account everything that needs to be included in your price. For companies that sell goods, this might include:

- performance and quality of the finished goods
- distribution capabilities
- service and installation.

For companies that sell a service, value factors might include:

- bottom-line impact of the service
- ability to meet tight deadlines
- experience level of staff delivering the service.

4 Pricing financially

After considering all the value factors, add up the direct costs incurred as a result of delivering the product, including labour and raw materials. Then add up all the indirect costs, such as rent, insurance and utilities.

Identify the profit the company needs to attain in order to fund new investment and reward employees. Forecast what the annual unit volumes will be. Divide the total costs and profits by the number of units sold annually to get a unit price. This kind of analysis will help ascertain where your prices should be set.

5 Pricing competitively

Studying your competitors is of course crucial, but do not simply copy them. Let them guide you in terms of where you set your boundaries. Examine the demand in the market:

- **Competitive analysis.** Look at the whole package offered by competitors. Are they serving price-conscious or affluent consumers? Are there any value-added services?

- **Ceiling price.** This is the highest price the market will bear. Survey experts and customers to determine pricing limits. The highest price in the market may not be the ceiling price.

- **Price elasticity.** This is the responsiveness of the demand for a good or service to the increase or decrease in its price. If the demand for your product is less elastic, you can set a higher ceiling on prices. Low elastic demand depends on a limited number of competitors, consumers' perception of quality, and the existence of consumers who do not seek the lowest price.

Once you understand the demand structure in your industry, review your costs and profit goals as set out in business or financial plans. Continue to gather competitive pricing information from sources such as intermediaries (distributors or brokers) and previous and prospective customers. Information on the price range of your competitors together with your own financial prices will give you two reference points for price setting.

6 Pricing by position

The last step is to consider how you want your products and services to be perceived in your market. Remember that the prices you set play a part in positioning the product and influencing customer perceptions. From the many pricing strategies available consider these three:

- Premium Price – the most expensive third of your market
- Middle Market Prices – the middle third
- Budget Price – the least expensive third.

The following matrix illustrates how quality and price influence perceptions.

	High price	Medium price	Low price
High quality	Premium	High value	Excellent value
Medium quality	Overpriced	Middle value	Good value
Low quality	Very overpriced	Overpriced	Economy

Based on the value factors identified, decide which of these three price levels best matches your product.

7 Parity pricing

Parity pricing is where businesses examine the competition and set their prices according to the market rate. When consumers see two similar products with the same price they consider them as equal, which means that the products are competitors and profits will decrease. Similarly, a lower price implies an inferior product and a higher price typically signals a superior product.

8 Cost-plus pricing

Cost-plus pricing is the determination of price by adding up the costs and then adding a profit margin. This strategy is especially prevalent among companies that are concerned with gross profit margins. Cost-plus pricing is easy to calculate, requires little information and is easy to administer. To arrive at a price, first calculate the cost of the product and then include an additional amount to represent profit. Though cost-plus pricing is a common method used by companies to determine prices, it has disadvantages such as not taking into account market prices or demand. It also provides few incentives for efficiency and tends to ignore the role of both consumers and competitors.

9 Variable cost pricing

With variable cost pricing (also known as marginal cost pricing), prices are set in relation to the variable costs of production (that is, ignoring fixed costs and overheads). This is done to achieve a contribution towards fixed costs and profit. Prices are set using variable costing by determining a target contribution per unit which reflects:

- variable costs per unit
- total fixed costs
- the desired level of target profit (i.e. contribution less fixed costs).

The advantages of using a variable/marginal costing method for pricing include:

- enabling short-term decision-making
- avoiding having to make an arbitrary allocation of fixed costs and overheads
- focusing the business on what is required to break even.

However, there are some potential disadvantages in using this method:

- there is a risk that the price set will not recover total fixed costs in the long term; ultimately, businesses must price their products to reflect the total costs of the business
- it may be difficult to raise prices if the contribution per unit is set too low.

10 Align price with the product life cycle

How high or low you set your prices will also be driven by where the product is in its life cycle. In general, the farther the product is through the life cycle, the lower the price should be, since by this stage the market will be saturated and price sensitivity will have increased with greater knowledge of the product. One technique to consider is removing the costs of support, training and services from the product, allowing you to lower the price without discounting.

11 Avoid a price war

A price war can wreak havoc, as margins are cut leaving businesses struggling to make a profit. To avoid a price war, consider the following:

- **Enhance exclusivity.** Products that are exclusive to your business provide protection from falling prices.

- **Drop high-maintenance goods.** There may be products or services in your business that have high customer-service and maintenance costs. Drop the unprofitable lines by finding out what customers do not want.

- **Add value.** Find out what value can be added to your business to make it stand out in the marketplace. Be the best business in the category.

- **Develop a brand name.** Businesses with strong brands are well placed to beat the competition.

As a manager you should avoid:

- neglecting to develop a pricing policy to guide pricing decisions
- copying the competition rather than simply taking it into account
- failing to take steps to avoid a price war that could damage both your business and that of your competitors and devalue the marketplace.

Effective purchasing

Effective purchasing is about buying the right goods and services at the right time, at the right price, in the right quantity and of the quality required to enable an organisation to achieve its objectives and fulfil its commitments. Effective purchasing maximises efficiency and is consistent with the organisation's overall strategy.

This checklist aims to help managers responsible for purchasing to adopt an effective strategy and to develop cooperative and mutually beneficial relationships with suppliers. It presents a proactive approach to purchasing and is intended to outline the major issues to be considered rather than provide details of the administration of purchase-order processes. Although it is aimed at those involved in centralised purchasing, the principles apply equally to decentralised buying.

An effective purchasing strategy:

- adds value for the organisation through efficiency and cost savings
- ensures the timely availability and quality of goods required by the organisation
- creates good relationships with suppliers based on trust
- balances controls and risks in the procurement process
- supports payment and accounting processes
- leads to a better understanding of the marketplace.

Action checklist: your organisation

1 Understand your organisation

Take the time to learn about how your own organisation functions and what is important to each department in terms of the supply of goods and services. What are the most crucial aspects for each line manager in terms of quality, price and delivery? Which items do they purchase most often and what are they used for? How does each department determine its reorder levels? Gather as much data as you can to provide a sound basis for formulating your strategy. It will also serve to demonstrate professionalism to your internal customers and increase their sense of involvement in the process.

2 Compile a purchase history

Use purchase orders and requisitions to compile a purchase history. Gather data on product types, order quantities, lead times, pricing and order frequency. Use the data to discover the purchasing patterns for key items. Pay particular attention to purchases that have been incurred by one department and charged to another.

3 Use the purchase history to become a proactive buyer

A clear understanding of the purchase history will enable you to negotiate better deals with suppliers by giving them an indication of the volumes they can expect you to acquire over the year. Anticipate reorder dates and do the groundwork in advance. Reduce delivery charges by ordering similar products at the same time. Arrange for suppliers to stock frequently used items free of charge, thus reducing your storage requirements, controlling lead times and providing the benefit of bulk purchasing. Monitor price fluctuations for seasonal trends.

4 Define and communicate your strategy

Make sure that your procurement strategy is clearly defined and communicated to all managers and directors. Consider whether decentralised arrangements could be helpful, weighing increased risks against potential cost and efficiency improvements. Set out your budget targets for the year ahead and the improvements that are required in areas such as order handling and efficiency. Devise an action plan for implementation and make sure that the targets are built into individual and departmental objectives.

Action checklist: your suppliers

1 Evaluate potential suppliers

Find out all you can about potential suppliers. Undertake company searches and review company accounts and annual reports. Examine their websites and product catalogues and ask to see samples where appropriate. Take up references and try to identify buyers in organisations similar to your own who can give feedback on supplier performance.

Areas to cover include:

- turnover and profitability
- how long the company has been trading
- who the major customers are
- whether the company is reliant on one major customer and what might happen if this account is lost
- what percentage of their turnover your business will generate
- who their manufacturers are and where they operate
- whether the company has any third-party certification, such as ISO 9000
- standard terms of trading and warranties
- terms relating to deliveries and shipments
- quality control policy
- ethical and environmental policies
- procedures for handling customer complaints

- invoicing and administrative procedures
- levels of insurance cover.

2 Visit potential suppliers

Visit suppliers wherever possible and ask for a tour of their premises, including the works and warehousing facilities. Find out who would be dealing with your orders and how they would be processed. Ask to meet the people with whom you would have day-to-day contact.

3 Develop positive relationships

Developing constructive relationships with your suppliers will help to make sure that you get the best deals and the best service. View your suppliers as partners and treat them with respect. Take an interest in your suppliers' business and the things that may affect their performance. For example:

- Have they won or lost any major contracts?
- How are they affected by the state of the economy?
- Will transport costs increase as a result of rising fuel prices?
- Will the price of paper materially affect a major print job scheduled for the end of the year?

Take account of any challenges or difficulties they face and be prepared to help where possible. Can you pre-purchase goods to minimise the effect of price rises, for example? Find out about their areas of expertise and take advantage of their specialist knowledge. They may be able to obtain goods that they don't normally hold at advantageous rates.

4 Maintain good communication

Good communication is a fundamental building block of constructive relationships. You expect your suppliers to keep you advised of delivery dates and any problems associated with your orders, so make sure that you reciprocate. Advise them if you are expecting a sudden decrease in purchases or, indeed, an increased requirement. Just as you should tell them exactly what you want of them, get them to tell you precisely what they expect of you.

Talk to senior managers and keep in regular contact with them. Get to know those you deal with as human beings. It is much easier to deal with matters (especially tricky ones) when you know the person you are talking to. However, do not allow personal considerations to outweigh business considerations.

5 Audit your major suppliers

Perform regular audits of your suppliers to assess their continued level of performance. Do they still meet the criteria you established when placing the first order? What improvement or deterioration in standards have you noticed in the service since then?

6 Maintain a competitive element

Conduct regular reviews of the prices and service you are getting from your suppliers. Make sure they understand that they have to remain competitive. Keep up-to-date with pricing and discount structures and be prepared to make suggestions that will help you get a better deal in the future. Customers can influence pricing policies, so make sure that the price you get represents good value for your organisation.

However, do not take a heavy-handed approach, dictate terms on a take-it-or-leave-it basis, or try to exploit your suppliers. Be open to negotiation. For audit purposes, retain documentation which shows that you have sought alternative prices.

7 Compare quotations

When considering quotes, make sure that you are comparing like with like. Check exclusions such as delivery, installation, training and insurance. Check the contract period, renewal dates and how long the price cited will be held. In the case of long-term contracts, consider what provision is made to hold prices at the current level or in line with increases in the retail price index. What are the payment terms?

8 Keep up to date with the marketplace

Visiting trade exhibitions and reading trade journals are important ways of keeping up to date with what is on offer in the marketplace. Online demonstrations, presentations and podcasts are also helpful in informed purchasing. These can save a lot of time providing you filter invitations carefully to identify the most relevant to your business.

9 Negotiate when the price must rise

If price rises are inevitable, try to negotiate alternative benefits, such as longer payment terms, prompt-payment discounts, quarterly as opposed to monthly invoicing, management reports, price stability for a fixed period, free delivery or increased delivery frequency. It may be possible to negotiate benefits even after orders have gone through and invoices have been received. Remember, the supplier wants to keep your business and may be able to help in other ways. Don't forget to negotiate terms for ongoing services, such as maintenance.

Action checklist: general good practice

1 Establish a code of ethics

- Use the same timescales for requesting payments from your customers and for making payments to your suppliers. Don't borrow long and lend short.

- Respect confidentiality – do not disclose suppliers' prices and methods of trading to competitors.

- Declare any personal interest.

- Do not accept gifts from suppliers or potential suppliers. It is good practice to advise all suppliers of this in writing when you commence trading with them, and especially before the Christmas period when most suppliers traditionally bear gifts.

2 Fulfil your side of the contract

Take care to place orders in good time. Make sure that they are timely and accurate and that invoices are promptly checked and payment approved by the due dates. Make sure payments are made on time in accordance with your agreement and that settlement discounts are correctly and promptly deducted. If you have a rollover contract, make sure that you know how much notice is required, should you wish to terminate the contract.

3 Maintain an audit trail

Maintain an audit trail of all purchase documents. Check orders, invoices and deliveries to make sure that:

- supplier accounts are not incorrectly set up or modified, resulting in false payments
- orders are not made for goods that are not required
- purchase-order requisitions are authentic – make enquiries if there is the least doubt
- excessive charges have not been made – particularly when published price lists are not available
- invoices are matched against purchase-order requisitions
- duplicate invoices are not received, resulting in duplicate payments
- automated advance payments are not made for goods or services that have not been received
- quantities received are correctly input on goods received notes
- goods received are exactly what was ordered and not cheaper substitutes
- returns and credit notes are dealt with promptly
- orders and invoices are not lost or misplaced through incorrect filing

- all records are accurate and up-to-date.

4 Manage purchasing risks

Identify risks related to the procurement process. Risks to consider include:

- overstocking and inflated inventory
- purchase of unsuitable goods or services
- shortages or misallocation of stock
- price fluctuations
- the risk of fraud through inadequate budgetary controls
- incomplete or incorrect paperwork and records
- the loss of data through computer failure
- risks associated with your company's reputation with regard to suppliers and customers or clients.

Maintain a register of risks, score them at regular intervals and keep the register up to date.

Make sure that your financial approval policy is sound, so that any errors or inflated charges are detected by the purchasing manager. Effective budgetary controls that assign appropriate levels of authority to managers and other staff involved in making purchases act as a barrier to fraud and corruption. Weak budgetary controls may allow fraud – for example, when costs have been allowed in the budget but allocated purchases are not required, when overruns are concealed or transferred, or when purchases are charged back to other departments.

As a manager you should avoid:

- allowing yourself to be dragged into a bidding war by suppliers
- making assumptions – make sure all details are clarified in writing, even if only by fax or email
- exceeding the limits of your authority

- staying with the same supplier 'because we've always used them' – be sure they are being used because they are the best
- moving to another supplier because of a minor dispute when the existing supplier is reliable and competitive.

Acknowledgements

The Chartered Management Institute (CMI) would like to thank the members of our Subject Matter Experts group for their generous contribution to the development of the management checklists. This panel of over 60 members and fellows of CMI and its sister institute, the Institute of Consulting, draw on their knowledge and expertise to provide feedback on the currency, relevance and practicality of the advice given in the checklists. A full listing of the subject matter experts is available at www.managers.org.uk/subject-matter-experts.

This book has been made possible by the work of CMI's staff, in particular Catherine Baker, Piers Cain, Sarah Childs, Michelle Jenkins, Linda Lashbrooke, Robert Orton, Nick Parker, Karen Walsh and not least Mary Wood, the Series Editor. We would also like to thank Stephen Brough, Paul Forty and Clare Grist Taylor of Profile Books for their support.

The management checklists are based on resources available online at www.managers.org.uk to CMI members to assist them in their work and career development, and to subscribers to the online resource portal ManagementDirect.

Index